Praise for *Meaningful Classroom Management*

"I can confidently say that there are many teachers and school leaders out there who have been waiting for a book like this. Classroom management continues to be a widespread topic of concern in education spaces. What Dr. Eakins has done that distinguishes his book from so many of the current texts is that he's putting an emphasis on culture and community, which are absolutely essential to any classroom management success."

—**Principal Baruti Kafele**, retired principal, education consultant, author

"In *Meaningful Classroom Management*, Sheldon Eakins invites teachers to rethink discipline, structure, and engagement through the lens of connection. With powerful personal stories, ready-to-use strategies, and proven frameworks, Eakins shows how centering community over individualism transforms classrooms into spaces where students feel safe, respected, and inspired to learn. Whether you're a first-year teacher or a seasoned veteran, this is your road map to creating a classroom culture that works."

—**Mary Rice-Boothe**, author of *Leading Within Systems of Inequity in Education*

"Dr. Eakins's positive and community-oriented approach to classroom management is one that can help both teachers and their students thrive. This book makes a compelling case for the importance of classroom culture and community—and more importantly, provides educators with actionable strategies they can use to help all students feel welcomed, valued, and empowered. I encourage every educator to read this book!"

—**Robert Barnett**, co-founder, Modern Classrooms Project

"This book is a must-read for educators who want to create learning environments that work for *everyone*. With ready-to-use strategies, case studies, and reflection protocols, Eakins invites us to be more intentional about classroom culture, honoring the full range of student backgrounds, strengths, and needs, including those from both individualistic and collectivist cultural traditions. At the heart is elevating your Teacher VIBE: Valuing Inclusion and Belonging for Everyone."

—**Katie Novak**, EdD, inclusion advocate, educational consultant, and bestselling author of 16 books, including *UDL Now!* and *Equity by Design*

"*Meaningful Classroom Management* offers a highly practical and culturally responsive pathway to deepening student engagement. It provides dozens of strategies to transform classroom environments into places where all students feel a strong sense of belonging and thrive. This book will also equip you with an easy-to-implement road map for building a cohesive and vibrant classroom community."

—**Ari Gerzon-Kessler**, author of *On the Same Team: Bringing Educators and Underrepresented Families Together*

"Sheldon Eakins writes from a place of deep knowing. This work calls educators to examine where we build from, how we design spaces of learning, and what legacy we leave in young minds. The shift from classroom management to classroom community requires courage, intention, and clarity about who we're serving. Eakins provides the road map. The rest is up to us."

—**Shawna Wells**, CEO, 7Gen Legacy Group

"The personal anecdotes, real-life experiences, and well-grounded research make this book a powerful resource. Dr. Eakins masterfully clarifies the true meaning of culture—beyond, yet inclusive of, race, gender, and ethnicity. At a time when myths about culture, cultural competency, and cultural awareness are widespread, *Meaningful Classroom Management* provides tangible strategies that educators at every level can put into practice to ensure that all students are seen, valued, and heard."

—**Dr. ClauDean Kizart**, educator and author of *Beyond Implicit and Explicit Biases: Healing the Root Causes of Inequity in Education*

MEANINGFUL CLASSROOM MANAGEMENT

SHELDON L. EAKINS

MEANINGFUL CLASSROOM MANAGEMENT

Adapting Your Teaching
to Build Culture and Community

Arlington, Virginia USA

2111 Wilson Boulevard, Suite 300 • Arlington, VA 22201 USA
Phone: 800-933-2723 or 703-578-9600
Website: www.ascd.org • Email: member@ascd.org
Author guidelines: www.ascd.org/write

Richard Culatta, *Chief Executive Officer;* Anthony Rebora, *Chief Content Officer;* Genny Ostertag, *Managing Director, Book Acquisitions & Editing;* Bill Varner, *Senior Acquisitions Editor;* Mary Beth Nielsen, *Director, Book Editing;* Liz Wegner, *Editor;* Lisa Hill, *Graphic Designer;* Circle Graphics, *Typesetter;* Kelly Marshall, *Production Manager;* Shajuan Martin, *E-Publishing Specialist;* Christopher Logan, *Senior Production Specialist*

Copyright © 2026 ASCD. All rights reserved. It is illegal to reproduce copies of this work in print or electronic format (including reproductions displayed on a secure intranet or stored in a retrieval system or other electronic storage device from which copies can be made or displayed) without the prior written permission of the publisher. By purchasing only authorized electronic or print editions and not participating in or encouraging piracy of copyrighted materials, you support the rights of authors and publishers. Readers who wish to reproduce or republish excerpts of this work in print or electronic format may do so for a small fee by contacting the Copyright Clearance Center (CCC), 222 Rosewood Dr., Danvers, MA 01923, USA (phone: 978-750-8400; fax: 978-646-8600; web: www.copyright.com). To inquire about site licensing options or any other reuse, contact ASCD Permissions at www.ascd.org/permissions or permissions@ascd.org. For a list of vendors authorized to license ASCD ebooks to institutions, see www.ascd.org/epubs. Send translation inquiries to translations@ascd.org.

ASCD® is a registered trademark of Association for Supervision and Curriculum Development. All other trademarks contained in this book are the property of, and reserved by, their respective owners, and are used for editorial and informational purposes only. No such use should be construed to imply sponsorship or endorsement of the book by the respective owners.

All web links in this book are correct as of the publication date below but may have become inactive or otherwise modified since that time. If you notice a deactivated or changed link, please email books@ascd.org with the words "Link Update" in the subject line. In your message, please specify the web link, the book title, and the page number on which the link appears.

PAPERBACK ISBN: 978-1-4166-3402-7   ASCD product #126017   n11/25
PDF EBOOK ISBN: 978-1-4166-3403-4; see Books in Print for other formats.
Quantity discounts are available: email programteam@ascd.org or call 800-933-2723, ext. 5773, or 703-575-5773. For desk copies, go to www.ascd.org/deskcopy.

Library of Congress Cataloging-in-Publication Data
Names: Eakins, Sheldon L. author
Title: Meaningful classroom management : adapting your teaching to build culture and community / Sheldon L. Eakins.
Description: Arlington, VA : ASCD, [2026] | Includes bibliographical references and index.
Identifiers: LCCN 2025030771 (print) | LCCN 2025030772 (ebook) |
  ISBN 9781416634027 paperback | ISBN 9781416634034 pdf
Subjects: LCSH: Classroom management | Classroom environment | Effective teaching
Classification: LCC LB3013 .E25 2026 (print) | LCC LB3013 (ebook)
LC record available at https://lccn.loc.gov/2025030771
LC ebook record available at https://lccn.loc.gov/2025030772

---

35 34 33 32 31 30 29 28 27 26   1 2 3 4 5 6 7 8 9 10 11 12

MEANINGFUL CLASSROOM MANAGEMENT

Introduction: Bridging Cultures in the Classroom 1

1. Exploring Classroom Dynamics 17

2. Rethinking Classroom Management 42

3. Mastering Classroom Observations with the Teacher LENS 70

4. Incorporating Teaching Techniques for Today's Classroom 94

5. Boosting Learning with Peer Assessments 135

6. Building Relationships Through Empathy 163

7. A Call for Adaptive Teaching 182

Acknowledgments 189

References 191

Index 195

About the Author 200

Introduction: Bridging Cultures in the Classroom

The year was 1999. I was in the 10th grade at a brand-new school, standing nervously in front of about a dozen high school students who were members of the school's theater club. I was auditioning to join their ranks. The director was there, observing quietly as I scanned the room, my palms sweaty and trembling. The pressure to do well felt immense, as my older sister had graduated the year before and left behind an impressive legacy in the same club. Part of me thought, *I've got this—I'm her younger brother, after all.* But deep down, I knew I would still have to prove myself.

At that point, I didn't have much acting experience. I vaguely recalled performing a monologue at a church talent show when I was younger, but that was about it. What I didn't know—though I wish someone had told me—was that the theater club had a tradition. During auditions, the director instructed the members to keep a straight face and not laugh, no matter what.

Completely unaware of this, I entered the audition with all the enthusiasm I could muster. The first prompt? "Act like a dog." I got down on all fours, barked, and committed to the role wholeheartedly. But instead of laughter or encouragement, I was met with stone-cold silence. It was crickets in the room. My confidence sank. I thought, *Oh no. I'm making a complete fool of myself.*

They asked me to try other prompts and improv exercises, but I knew I wasn't doing well. My mind raced, and every move

I made felt forced. When the director eventually released the list of students who made the team, I wasn't surprised that my name wasn't on it. I had bombed that audition, plain and simple.

But that experience taught me an invaluable lesson about my personal strengths and preferences. Improvisation wasn't for me. Improv, with its emphasis on creative spontaneity and expressing ideas without the constraints of a script, scared me. What I needed was structure—lines to learn, parts to rehearse, and a clear framework to follow before stepping into the spotlight.

So why does this experience matter, and how does it relate to the classroom?

Finding My Strengths

As an adult, I find myself on stage all the time. I have no fear of giving keynotes, speaking in public, presenting, or conducting workshops. In these settings, I can be charismatic, witty, and engaging. I know how to invoke emotions, and I consider myself a skilled storyteller. As a school principal, I've led staff meetings and proudly promoted my school within the community. The difference between these moments and that high school audition? Preparation.

Improvisation relies on spontaneity and independence. But these traits conflict with my natural preference for group harmony, preparation, and maintaining unified rules and structure. So how does this distinction relate to the classroom?

As educators, we must recognize that each student has their own unique way of showcasing their abilities. It's our responsibility to create an environment that honors and nurtures the individual strengths of every student. Not every child will thrive under the same conditions or respond well to the same pressures.

Some students might shine in group settings, whereas others may excel when given more autonomy and opportunities for personal creativity. By offering a variety of ways to demonstrate learning, and understanding that success looks different for every student, we can help them discover their voice and bring out their best.

Culture Versus Learning Styles: Understanding the Distinction

It's easy to confuse cultural influences with learning styles, but they are not the same. For years, the idea of *learning styles*—that individuals learn best when instruction is matched to a preferred modality such as visual, auditory, kinesthetic, or reading/writing—was widely accepted. However, a growing body of research has since debunked this theory, finding no consistent evidence that tailoring instruction to a so-called "learning style" improves outcomes (Kirschner, 2017).

Although students may express preferences for how they engage with content, it is neither practical nor necessary to design lessons solely based on these preferences. What matters is how students' cultural backgrounds and lived experiences shape the ways they make sense of and engage with learning (Hammond, 2015).

Culture is a broader framework that shapes not just preferences but also expectations, behaviors, and classroom interactions. It influences how students perceive authority, how they collaborate or work independently, how they respond to feedback, and their approach to problem solving.

For example, a student who thrives on structured, highly detailed assignments may not simply have a personal preference for order; their success could reflect a cultural background that values precision, hierarchy, and careful planning. Conversely, a student who struggles with quiet, independent work might not be distracted or disengaged; they may come from a culture where learning is interactive, communal, and based on collective meaning-making.

If teachers interpret these behaviors only through the outdated lens of learning styles, they risk overlooking deeper cultural factors that shape engagement. Understanding this distinction is key. A student's approach to education isn't just about how they absorb information; it's about the values they've internalized from their family, community, and broader environment.

By recognizing these cultural contexts, educators can move beyond surface-level teaching adjustments and design learning environments that validate, support, and uplift all students.

Understanding Culture in Education

Culture has a huge impact on our preferred performance styles. Let's dive deeper into this topic.

What comes to mind when I say the phrase "culture in education"? For many people, their first thoughts are about race and ethnicity. Although those are important aspects of culture, focusing solely on them can narrow our perspective and limit our understanding of what culture truly is.

In today's political climate, discussing culture in education can make some teachers uncomfortable. Conversations about diversity, equity, and inclusion often evoke defensiveness, especially when people feel the topic is focused on race. I've led workshops on cultural competency, helping educators reflect on how their own backgrounds relate to their students' experiences. Sometimes I hear responses like "Why do we have to talk about this? Why can't we just teach people to be nice to everyone?"

But avoiding conversations about culture does a disservice to our students.

Broadening the Definition of Culture

The word *culture* isn't a bad word, but it can carry negative connotations because it's often misunderstood. Many people limit the concept of culture to just race and ethnicity. Pairing the word *culture* with anything related to diversity, equity, inclusion, and belonging can cause tensions to arise quickly. However, culture is much more than race and ethnicity. It includes the shared values, beliefs, customs, and behaviors that shape how individuals see and interact with the world (Hofstede et al., 2010).

We all have culture. We share values, beliefs, customs, and behaviors with the people we're closest to. As educators, we must broaden our understanding of culture to include its many layers and elements. These layers influence how students learn, communicate, and behave in the classroom. When we understand culture in its broader sense, we create classrooms that are more inclusive and responsive to the needs of every student.

Culture isn't just a checkbox in discussions about diversity. It's an active force that shapes how students interact with their learning environment. For some students, education has always been framed through an individualist lens, prioritizing personal success over group success. Others may come from backgrounds where learning is a communal process, where knowledge is passed down through storytelling, mentorship, and collective engagement.

Understanding culture in education requires moving beyond surface-level assumptions. Too often, cultural discussions focus only on food, holidays, attire, and language rather than exploring the deeper layers of culture, such as values, communication styles, body language, and ways of processing information. These key characteristics shape how students respond to classroom expectations, engage in learning, and define success.

For example, students from collectivist cultures may be less inclined to seek individual recognition for their achievements, instead prioritizing group harmony and collaborative success. This inclination could be misinterpreted by teachers from individualistic backgrounds as a lack of confidence or motivation. On the other hand, students from individualistic cultures may naturally assert themselves in class discussions and advocate for their own learning needs, which might be perceived as overconfidence or self-centeredness by teachers who value a more communal approach.

Developing a Teacher LENS

By broadening our definition of culture to include these diverse learning perspectives, we cultivate more inclusive, responsive, and effective classrooms. This book is not just about culturally responsive teaching. It's about understanding how cultural norms influence learning preferences and how we, as educators, can create environments where every student can thrive.

To do this, teachers must develop a Teacher LENS: Look for biases, Examine verbal and nonverbal communication, Notice group dynamics, and Shift perspectives and interpret behavior. The Teacher LENS allows them to recognize and honor the different ways students engage with learning. Developing the Teacher LENS involves asking deeper questions, such as these:

- How does culture influence a student's preference for group work or independent study?

- How do cultural values shape a student's communication style—whether they speak up readily in class or prefer to listen first?
- How do students interpret feedback and authority based on their cultural background?

Incorporating cultural awareness into teaching practices goes beyond simply recognizing differences; it means creating instructional strategies and classroom policies that are flexible and adaptable to meet the needs of all students. Whether it's allowing students to choose between individual or group assessments, incorporating storytelling as a method of instruction, or structuring participation opportunities in a way that respects both direct and indirect communication styles, culturally responsive teaching requires intentionality and awareness. By expanding our understanding of culture, we ensure that classrooms become spaces where all students—not just those who align with the dominant cultural expectations—can thrive.

Before You Judge This Book . . .

Before you put this book down, donate it to the nearest thrift store, or—worse—consider adding it to the banned books list at your local school or library, I ask you to keep an open mind. This book is not what you may think it is.

Yes, we'll talk about how to consider the cultural backgrounds of your students and how to be culturally responsive. But the emphasis here is on something more specific: understanding how cultural norms influence the way students engage, learn, and express themselves. This book will help you recognize the differences between individualistic cultural norms and collectivist cultural norms—and how these differences show up in the classroom.

The Influence of Individualism in the United States

The United States has a strong focus on individualism, which shapes many areas of our society, including education, the workplace, and even our everyday interactions (Shin et al., 2020). Let's look at a few examples.

Social expectations

From a young age, people in the United States are encouraged to be independent and self-reliant. This message is reinforced through movies, TV shows, social media, and societal norms. For example, young adults are often expected to move out of their parents' homes, start careers, and build their own families. In fact, adults who still live with their parents are sometimes looked down upon, because independence is viewed as a key marker of success.

The self-help culture

The booming self-help industry in the United States reflects the cultural focus on personal responsibility. Countless books, seminars, and workshops promote personal growth. Stories of individuals overcoming adversity to "find themselves" or "be true to themselves" are celebrated in books, films, and media.

Emphasis on individual rights

The foundation of the United States is deeply rooted in individualistic cultural norms. The Bill of Rights is a clear example, emphasizing personal freedoms such as the right to free speech, assembly, and religion. These principles highlight the importance of protecting the individual over the collective.

Individualism in sports and entertainment

Individualism is also celebrated in sports and entertainment in the United States. Awards like the Grammys, Emmys, and Tonys honor personal accomplishments. In sports, titles like Most Valuable Player or Franchise Player highlight and reward individual excellence, even within team contexts.

Given this cultural backdrop, it's no surprise that individualism is deeply embedded in the United States' educational system as well. Let's take a closer look at the role it plays in that context.

Individualism in the Education System

The U.S. education system often emphasizes personal achievement over collective success. Students are encouraged to take initiative, lead projects, and assert themselves in classroom discussions. This emphasis is also reflected in the various ways we measure and evaluate performance, such as the following:

- **Report cards and grades:** Individual grades track each student's progress and achievements.
- **Parent–teacher conferences:** These meetings are designed to provide updates on a specific child's performance rather than group or community outcomes.
- **Standardized testing:** Students take standardized tests, and their scores are compared to the scores of their peers nationwide. High scores are celebrated, whereas low scores prompt concern and intervention.
- **GPA tracking:** In secondary education, students' academic performance is boiled down to a single number: their grade point average.

This focus on individual performance mirrors the broader societal value placed on independence and self-reliance in the United States. Although this approach works well for some, it may not suit every student. As we move forward, we'll explore how collectivist cultural norms contrast with this model—and how embracing both perspectives can create more inclusive classrooms.

> **Examples of Individualism in U.S. Schools**
> - Valedictorian/salutatorian designations
> - Standardized tests
> - GPAs, report cards
> - Academic celebrations
> - Scholarships

In education in the United States, students are often encouraged to outperform their peers and strive to be the best. Success is frequently measured by personal milestones such as earning scholarships, gaining admission to prestigious universities, or excelling in academics and extracurricular activities. Students are ranked and celebrated individually through honors like being designated valedictorian or salutatorian, included on the honor roll, or placed on the dean's list. These systems reinforce the idea that achievement is a personal endeavor, not a collective one.

Classrooms often emphasize individual work over group activities. Although collaborative assignments like project-based learning (PBL) are common, individual performance remains the gold standard for measuring success. For instance, standardized tests such as the ACT or the SAT are designed for solo performance; there's no collaborative format. Even accommodations for students with special needs focus on individual adjustments, such as extra time, rather than offering opportunities for group-based success.

Although collaborative learning is sometimes incorporated as part of a formative assessment, standardized testing and grading prioritize individual efforts. In these scenarios, working together—something that might come naturally to students from collectivist cultures—is often labeled as "cheating."

The Impact of Individualism on Collectivist Cultures

The strong emphasis on individual achievement in schools can create challenges for students from collectivist backgrounds, where group harmony, cooperation, and mutual support are highly valued. In classrooms that prioritize individual performance, these students may feel uncomfortable or out of place. Activities such as solo presentations or competitive tasks can be particularly stressful, because they contrast sharply with students' cultural preference for group-based achievements. This disconnect can result in stress, less participation, and even a sense of alienation when their preference for group work and collective success is overlooked.

Reflecting on my own experience auditioning for the theater group in high school, I now recognize how my collectivist tendencies played a role. I struggled with the audition because it required me to stand out individually, perform solo, and compete without any guidance or structure. Tasks like this didn't align with my natural inclinations. Instead, I thrived in choir—a space where my preference for group harmony felt valued and where collaboration was central to success.

The Misunderstood Silence

As educators, we often talk about making sure every student participates and every voice is heard. Strategies like pulling names from a cup or using popsicle sticks to randomly select students to speak are intended to ensure fairness. However, for students from collectivist cultures, this approach can feel uncomfortable.

Imagine calling on a student only to see them hesitate, appearing unprepared or even distressed. That hesitation isn't necessarily due to a lack of engagement or understanding. In collectivist cultures, valued behaviors include listening, observing, and speaking only when doing so benefits the group. Students from collectivist cultures may prefer to process information quietly, organize their thoughts, and speak only when they feel ready to contribute meaningfully.

I deeply relate to this preference. I take notes and reflect before speaking because I want to ensure that my contributions are thoughtful and well-prepared. Extemporaneous conversation or speaking off the cuff is not my strength. Even as a keynote speaker, my confidence comes from preparation—doing my research and practicing my speeches. If I were asked to give an impromptu 30-minute talk, the experience would be vastly different.

The Pressure to Conform

Students from collectivist cultures often face an internal conflict between their cultural values and the dominant individualistic norms in U.S. schools. This tension can manifest as pressure to conform. For example, these students may feel compelled to avoid speaking their home language, wearing traditional attire, or eating culture-specific foods in public. Some may even adopt Americanized versions of their names to avoid standing out. In many households, parents might encourage their children to assimilate—advising them to "be quiet," "fit in," and adapt to the dominant culture.

This pressure to conform can lead to feelings of social isolation, as students may sense that their values and identities aren't understood or respected. Over time, the need to suppress their natural inclinations toward group-oriented behaviors can result in stress, anxiety, and even burnout.

The Need for Balance in Education

The favoring of individualistic norms in U.S. schools, often at the expense of students from collectivist cultures, creates an imbalance. This imbalance can affect not only the academic success of collectivist students but also their mental health and sense of belonging.

To address this possible consequence, educators must recognize these cultural differences and strive to create a balance between individualistic and collectivist approaches. By valuing both perspectives, educators can foster inclusive classrooms where students from diverse backgrounds feel seen, respected, and empowered to succeed without compromising their cultural identity.

Introducing *Meaningful Classroom Management*

Meaningful Classroom Management: Adapting Your Teaching to Build Culture and Community explores the intersection of classroom management and the cultural backgrounds of students—whether those backgrounds align with individualistic or collectivist values. This book is about bridging those differences to create classrooms that value every student.

Chapter 1: Exploring Classroom Dynamics

Cultural values, like individualism and collectivism, influence how students engage with content and how we, as educators, design our instructional practices. In this chapter, we explore how these values affect teaching and learning—whether students prefer working independently or in groups. By reflecting on your teaching practices and finding ways to balance individual work with group activities, you can create a classroom where every student feels they belong and has the opportunity to succeed.

Chapter 2: Rethinking Classroom Management

What if we thought of classroom management as building a supportive community rather than enforcing rules and compliance? In this chapter, I encourage you to rethink traditional approaches to behavior management and shift toward practices that prioritize inclusion and belonging for all students. Through strategies like collaborative classroom agreements and thoughtful seating arrangements, we can balance the needs of both individual and group-focused learners. I also introduce the Teacher VIBE mindset—Valuing Inclusion and Belonging for Everyone—as a guide to help you create culturally inclusive classrooms where all students feel accepted and empowered.

Chapter 3: Mastering Classroom Observations with the Teacher LENS

Observation is a powerful tool for understanding your students, especially when viewed through a cultural lens. In this chapter, I share the Teacher LENS framework, comprising the following components:

- Look for biases.
- Examine verbal and nonverbal communication.

- Notice group dynamics.
- Shift perspectives and interpret behavior.

Using this framework, I reflect on moments when my rigid classroom rules clashed with my students' cultural norms, leading to disengagement. For example, I came to see behaviors like talking during tasks or helping peers not as disruptions but as natural expressions of their cultural preferences. This chapter challenges teachers to confront biases, embrace cultural differences, and build classrooms that value diverse behaviors.

Chapter 4: Incorporating Teaching Techniques for Today's Classroom

Incorporating practices like project-based learning, storytelling, and gamification can transform classrooms into collaborative, engaging spaces. Just as *The Legend of Zelda* revolutionized gaming by introducing collective problem solving and the ability to save progress made from one session to another, these classroom practices can foster a sense of belonging and teamwork among students in the following ways:

- PBL can connect classroom content to students' lives.
- Storytelling can bridge cultural gaps by empowering students to share their identities.
- Gamification can blend individual achievements with group challenges, making learning fun and interactive.

These strategies celebrate diversity, strengthen community, and help every student feel valued in the learning process.

Chapter 5: Boosting Learning with Peer Assessments

Peer assessments are a powerful way to foster connection and empathy in the classroom. In this chapter, I show how creating a culture of trust and mutual respect empowers students to support one another through feedback methods like Glow and Grow or the Positive Sandwich. These practices reinforce collaboration and community for collectivist students, while individualistic students gain self-reflection and critical-thinking skills. Thoughtfully blending individual and group strengths creates a culturally inclusive environment where every student feels supported.

Chapter 6: Building Relationships Through Empathy

Empathy is the foundation of strong teacher–student relationships. In this chapter, I explore how empathy goes beyond understanding someone else's experience. It's about valuing and validating their unique backgrounds and emotions. By building emotional intelligence, recognizing biases, and understanding cultural dynamics, we can create classrooms where both collectivist and individualistic students feel seen and respected. Empathy, paired with strategies like group-centered learning and restorative practices, turns classrooms into inclusive spaces where every student can thrive.

Chapter 7: A Call for Adaptive Teaching

In the last chapter of the book, I call for adaptive teaching—creating classrooms where every student feels valued and included. Doing so requires balancing individual achievement with group success, embedding cultural awareness into daily practices, and shifting from compliance-based management to community-focused engagement. By adopting a Teacher VIBE and applying the Teacher LENS, you can create spaces where cultural differences become strengths. At the heart of this journey is empathy, guiding us to understand and honor each student's perspective. Adaptive teaching is a process, and even small changes can make a meaningful difference.

1

Exploring Classroom Dynamics

In most homes within the United States, the refrigerator stands out as more than just an appliance. It's a silent witness to the character and values of the family that fills it. Growing up, I realized that our refrigerator was no different. It was a place to keep our food cold, but it was also a snapshot of our family's daily life and cultural values. I grew up vegetarian and was raised not to eat certain types of meat, such as pork and shellfish. My siblings and I were taught that they were unclean, and to this day, even though I'm not as religiously observant anymore, I continue to abstain from pork and shellfish.

One thing that stands out about my childhood and our refrigerator was that we were blessed to always have a packed fridge. However, each item had a specific purpose. See, my mom was particular about what was in the fridge and how those items were allocated. She would tell us, "Don't touch this—it's for dinner tonight," or "That snack is for your brother." Of course, I had my favorites like orange juice and peanut butter, and the rest of the family knew those were the items I would favor. But even the items that I loved came with boundaries: one glass of juice per day, just a taste of peanut butter, no more. These rules weren't just about rationing food; they were lessons in personal boundaries and ownership, respect for individualism, and structured order and responsibility.

As I grew older and started my own family, I noticed a shift in how our household operated, particularly with something as simple as the refrigerator. In my childhood home, the fridge reflected structured individualism; specific items were assigned to particular people. If you wanted something, you checked first to ensure it wasn't someone else's. But in my adult household, the fridge became a communal space where everything was shared. The rule was simple: If you're hungry, eat what you find. Groceries were bought for everyone, and nothing was off-limits. Guests followed the same unspoken rule. If you saw a bag of chips, you didn't need to ask permission or wonder if it was labeled for someone else. It was understood that everything was for everyone.

This shift from individual ownership to collective sharing highlights the difference between individualistic and collectivist cultural norms. In an individualistic system, personal responsibility and ownership are prioritized. Everyone has their designated space and set of resources, and success is often measured by what one can achieve independently. In contrast, a collectivist approach emphasizes shared responsibility, interdependence, and communal comfort. Success is measured by the group's comfort rather than just the individual's.

This same contrast plays out in our classrooms every day. In many Western educational systems, students are expected to complete their work independently, excel on their own merits, and prove their individual abilities. Classroom structures often reinforce competition—individual grades, ranked achievements, and silent, solo work time. However, this approach may feel unfamiliar or even isolating for students from collectivist cultural backgrounds. They may be more comfortable in environments that encourage collaboration, shared learning, and group achievement. Just like the shift in my household dynamics, where food became a shared resource rather than an individually assigned one, teachers must recognize that some students come from cultural backgrounds where learning is a communal effort, not a solo endeavor.

Understanding these differences is critical. When a student moves around the classroom seeking help from peers instead of silently working alone, or when they hesitate to take personal credit for a group project, these behaviors shouldn't be seen as defiance or disengagement. They are reflections of deeply ingrained cultural norms. Without this awareness, teachers may unintentionally misinterpret a student's natural learning tendencies and impose disciplinary actions or make negative assumptions that hinder the student's educational experience.

By recognizing and valuing both individualistic and collectivist learning approaches, educators can create more inclusive classrooms that provide space for personal achievement and communal learning. The goal is not to replace one system with the other but to build an educational environment where all students, regardless of cultural background, can thrive.

The way something as ordinary as a refrigerator is managed can reveal much about cultural values. In my childhood, boundaries and individual portions were prioritized. In my adult home, shared resources and collective ownership took precedence.

Now, you might be wondering, *Why is he talking about refrigerators?* The answer is simple: Just as a refrigerator reflects cultural values in a household, the way we design and manage our classrooms reflects cultural values in education. These values shape everything, from how we structure assignments to how we interact with students and colleagues.

In this chapter, we'll explore why understanding these cultural nuances matters in the classroom. We'll start with a discussion of self-reflection, helping you identify where you fall on the individualist–collectivist spectrum in both life and teaching. Then, we'll examine examples of individualist and collectivist teaching practices, highlighting the risks of leaning too heavily in one direction. Finally, we'll explore strategies for achieving a balanced approach to instructional practice that fosters a sense of belonging for all students.

Different Learning Settings and Classroom Preferences

Let's begin with a little self-reflection. When it's time for professional development, how do you prefer to learn? Which of the following three possibilities best describes your preferred setting?

- You like to sit, listen, and absorb information. ("Just teach me what I don't know.")
- You prefer working in small groups, collaborating and discussing ideas with others.
- You thrive in a hands-on setting, engaging in activities like icebreakers or games.

When it comes to learning settings, your students are no different. Some prefer working independently, tackling assignments solo, with clear instructions. "Just give me the worksheet," they might say. Others thrive in group settings: "Pair me with a friend, and we'll knock this out," or "Let's form a group and figure it out together."

The same assignment can produce different outcomes depending on how it's presented and assessed. Let's explore this idea through a real-life classroom scenario.

A Classroom Scenario: Understanding Different Needs

Imagine this: Ms. Thompson, a middle school math teacher, hands out a worksheet at the start of class. The goal is to assess whether students understood yesterday's lesson.

"OK, class," she says. "Work on these problems independently and silently. When you're done, we'll go over the answers together."

As the students begin, Ms. Thompson notices that Jason, one of her more energetic students, doesn't seem focused. He gets up, walks around, and starts asking classmates, "Hey, what'd you get for number 5?"

Some students whisper back, "I got 7" or "I chose 316," while others shush him: "Go away! We're supposed to work alone!"

Ms. Thompson walks over, taps Jason on the shoulder, and quietly says, "Jason, please go back to your desk and finish the worksheet on your own." Jason complies, but within minutes, he's tapping his pencil on the desk, breaking the lead, and getting up to sharpen it. He fidgets, stares off into space, and clearly isn't engaged.

Addressing Behavioral Challenges in the Classroom

The scenario with Jason and Ms. Thompson illustrates a common challenge many educators face: a student who struggles to remain seated and complete their work. Jason represents the classic "can't sit still" child.

As educators, our response to this behavior often depends on the time of day, how our day is going, or our relationship with the student. A typical reaction might involve disciplinary action: a stern look, writing their name on the board, taking away privileges, or, in more extreme cases, removing them from the classroom.

But what happens when a child misses instructional time? Removal from the classroom creates more work for the teacher, who now needs to spend time reteaching and helping Jason catch up. Unfortunately, this follow-up doesn't always happen. Without reinforcement or restorative practices, students like Jason often fall through the cracks.

Over time, Jason might be labeled as a "troublemaker," a reputation that follows him not just through the school year but sometimes into the next grade. This label can affect how teachers view and treat him, perpetuating a cycle of disengagement and missed opportunities for learning.

Considering Alternative Approaches

Students like Jason—who arguably need the most support and attention—are often the ones most likely to disengage, struggle academically, and even drop out. Sadly, the "troublemaker" label can shape their school experience and their future.

In *Leading Equity: Becoming an Advocate for All Students* (2022), I discuss the "horn effect," which describes how negative perceptions of a student can unfairly influence how they're treated. When educators allow biases such as the horn effect to dictate their approach, students who need the most care and support often receive the least.

Let's revisit Jason's story. What if Ms. Thompson had approached the situation differently?

Understanding Jason's Needs

Why isn't Jason staying in his seat? Why does he seem disengaged or restless? These questions are critical for identifying the root of the problem. Here are a few possibilities:

- **Difficulty with the material.** Jason might find the content too challenging, leading to frustration and a lack of confidence in his ability to complete the task independently.
- **Lack of engagement.** The worksheet may not be stimulating enough to capture Jason's attention, prompting him to seek engagement in other ways.
- **Cultural mismatch.** Jason's behavior might reflect cultural values and learning preferences that differ from the classroom's expectations.

This last point is crucial. Jason's actions suggest he may come from a collectivist cultural background. If Ms. Thompson had recognized this key characteristic, she could have adjusted her approach to better meet his needs.

Jason's behavior in this scenario reflects several collectivist traits. For example, his preference for working with peers and seeking interaction rather than tackling the assignment alone may be tied to his cultural values. (I'll provide strategies later in the book to help you identify individualistic and collectivist tendencies in your classroom.)

By understanding Jason's cultural perspective, Ms. Thompson could have adapted her teaching approach to create a more inclusive and supportive learning environment—one that values collaboration and ensures students like Jason don't feel left out or misunderstood.

Alternative Strategies to Discipline

Addressing Jason's behavior through a more empathetic and culturally responsive lens can prevent disengagement and foster a supportive learning environment. Here are two strategies Ms. Thompson might consider as alternatives to traditional disciplinary actions.

Option 1: Group work

Jason is a high-energy, social learner who might thrive in a group setting rather than working independently. By assigning him to a small group, Ms. Thompson can channel his energy into productive collaboration with his peers.

Some teachers may hesitate to use group work, fearing it could lead to further disruptions or off-task behavior. Without proper protocols or consistent use of this format, these concerns are valid. However, with clear expectations and routines (covered in Chapter 4), group work can be an effective strategy.

Group work is especially beneficial for students who value collectivist cultural norms. It emphasizes teamwork, relationship building, and achieving shared goals. Rather than competing to finish first or get all the answers right, students collaborate to solve problems together. For example, if Jason knows the answer to problem number 5 but struggles with number 6, a group setting allows him to ask for help and receive support from his peers. This collaborative approach can reduce frustration and keep him motivated to engage with the task.

Option 2: Movement breaks

Sometimes students like Jason simply need a break. Ms. Thompson could address his restlessness by incorporating short movement breaks or classroom tasks, such as the following:

- Passing out papers or collecting assignments.
- Leading a quick physical activity (e.g., stretches or light exercises).
- Writing answers on the board during class discussions.

Movement breaks are culturally responsive because they reflect communal and relational aspects of collectivist values. For instance, allowing Jason to write answers on the board involves both physical activity and interaction with classmates. This option helps him feel like an active and valued part of the group.

Additionally, physical activities like leading a brief exercise session (e.g., 20 jumping jacks or 5 push-ups) can satisfy Jason's need for motion while reinforcing his connection to the class. These breaks not only redirect his energy but also align with his cultural preference for interdependence and teamwork.

Why do these options matter? By choosing group work and movement breaks, Ms. Thompson can meet Jason where he is, both behaviorally and culturally. Students from collectivist backgrounds often prioritize group harmony, interdependence, and community over individual competition. These strategies respect Jason's cultural values while addressing the root cause of his restlessness.

Integrating Cultural Awareness in the Classroom

Recognizing and honoring Jason's collectivist background enables Ms. Thompson to create a learning environment that respects his cultural identity while supporting his academic success. This approach reduces restlessness, enhances engagement, and fosters a sense of belonging.

You might be wondering, *Why does collectivism matter so much? What does it have to do with culture?* Let's dive into the research to unpack this concept and explore how it connects to classroom dynamics.

Hofstede's Cultural Dimensions Model

In the late 1970s, a Dutch psychologist named Geert Hofstede introduced a groundbreaking framework to help us understand cultural differences across societies. Based on his research with IBM employees in more than 50 countries, Hofstede (2001) identified the following set of six cultural dimensions that distinguish one culture from another:

- Individualism versus collectivism
- Power distance
- Masculinity versus femininity
- Uncertainty avoidance
- Long-term versus short-term orientation
- Indulgence versus restraint

Among these dimensions, individualism versus collectivism is particularly relevant to education, as it measures the degree to which individuals are integrated into groups and how that shapes their behaviors, values, and priorities (Hofstede et al., 2010).

Individualistic societies emphasize personal achievements, individual rights, competition, and independence. People are encouraged to prioritize their own goals and make decisions for themselves. By contrast, collectivist societies focus on group loyalty and harmony, placing the needs of the group above individual desires. Figure 1.1 compares the characteristics of individualism and collectivism.

What's fascinating about Hofstede's framework is that the United States ranks highest in individualism among the more than 50 countries he studied, scoring 91 out of 100. This cultural

FIGURE 1.1
Hofstede's Comparison of Individualism Versus Collectivism

Individualism	Collectivism
• Self-reliance	• Group reliance
• Personal goals prioritized	• Group goals prioritized
• Emphasis on individual rights	• Emphasis on community and harmony
• Independence valued	• Interdependence valued
• Personal achievements highlighted	• Group achievements highlighted
• Direct communication	• Indirect communication
• Individual decision making	• Consensus decision making

orientation is reflected in many aspects of American life, including education, where individual achievement is a cornerstone.

Countries including Australia and Great Britain also lean heavily toward individualism. On the other end of the spectrum, collectivist cultures include Hong Kong, Serbia, Malaysia, and Portugal, where group goals and harmony take precedence.

Hofstede's insights inspired me to explore how these cultural orientations influence teaching practices. When I started to examine classroom dynamics through this lens, it became clear that cultural values play a significant role in shaping both student behavior and instructional strategies.

Reflecting on Your Teaching Practices and Developing Self-Awareness

Have you reflected on your current teaching practices? Do they tend to favor individualism over collectivism?

Whether you're a veteran teacher, a first-year educator, or somewhere in between, there's always room to improve. That growth starts with reflection—understanding how your cultural orientation affects the way you interact with others and, ultimately, how you lead your classroom.

We work in diverse educational environments, filled with students who bring unique characteristics, languages, and talents into our classrooms. It's vital to reflect on whether our cultural orientations—individualistic or collectivist—influence our expectations, perceptions of student behavior, and approach to how we set up our classroom environments.

Any effort to better support your students must start with self-awareness. Understanding whether you naturally lean toward individualism or collectivism can offer valuable insights into how your background and preferences align—or sometimes clash—with the cultural values of the students in your classroom. By beginning with self-awareness, you equip yourself with the tools to be a more culturally responsive educator.

A Self-Assessment Tool

To guide you in reflecting on your cultural orientation, I've created the self-assessment tool presented in Figure 1.2. The purpose of this assessment isn't to label or categorize yourself but to deepen your understanding of your values, how they influence your teaching, and how you can create a classroom environment where every student feels valued and supported. By examining your tendencies in areas like independence, collaboration, personal achievement, and group harmony, you'll begin to see how these values shape your classroom environment. The insights you gain are meant to serve as an initial spark for further learning and reflection. Growth within your instructional practices begins with an honest look at your current methods. Ultimately, I hope the process presented in Figure 1.2 helps you better understand who you are, what you value, and how those values influence your interactions with students.

FIGURE 1.2
Self-Assessment for Cultural Awareness

Instructions
This self-assessment tool is designed to help you reflect on your personal cultural orientation. For each statement below, rate how strongly you agree or disagree, using the following scale:

1 = Strongly Disagree
2 = Disagree
3 = Neutral
4 = Agree
5 = Strongly Agree

After completing the self-assessment, tally your scores to determine your orientation toward individualism or collectivism.

Statement	Score
Section 1: Individualistic Leaning	
1. I prefer to set personal goals and work independently to achieve them.	
2. I believe in standing out and being recognized for my individual achievements.	
3. I value personal autonomy and the ability to make my own decisions.	
4. I feel more comfortable working alone rather than relying on others.	
5. I prioritize my personal needs and desires over those of the group.	
6. I believe that success is defined by individual accomplishments rather than group achievements.	
7. I prefer to express my own opinions and ideas, even if they differ from those of the majority.	
8. I find it important to take responsibility for my own actions and outcomes.	
Section 2: Collectivist Leaning	
9. I feel a strong sense of belonging and loyalty to my family, community, or team.	
10. I believe that group harmony and consensus are more important than personal opinions.	
11. I prefer to work collaboratively with others rather than independently.	

(continued)

FIGURE 1.2
Self-Assessment for Cultural Awareness *(Continued)*

Statement	Score
12. I often consider how my actions will affect the group before making decisions.	
13. I value the success of the group or team over my personal success.	
14. I feel responsible for the well-being of others in my community or group.	
15. I prefer to conform to group norms and expectations rather than stand out.	
16. I feel a sense of responsibility for ensuring that everyone in my group or community succeeds.	

Scoring
    Individualistic Orientation Score:
        Add up your scores for statements 1–8: ____
    Collectivist Orientation Score:
        Add up your scores for statements 9–16: ____

Interpretation
    High Individualistic Score (32–40): You probably value being independent, focusing on your own achievements and being self-reliant.
    Moderate Individualistic Score (24–31): You prefer being independent but also see the importance of working with others in some situations.
    Balanced Score (17–23): You value both personal success and working well with others, finding a good balance between the two.
    Moderate Collectivist Score (24–31): You lean toward teamwork and group goals but still appreciate your independence.
    High Collectivist Score (32–40): You likely value teamwork and group success more than individual achievements, focusing on harmony and collaboration.

Reflection Questions
- How does your cultural orientation affect how you get along with others?
- How does your orientation align or conflict with your current work environment?
- How can you use this self-awareness to enhance your effectiveness in collaborative or independent settings?

How Cultural Responsiveness Can Develop

As noted, completing a self-assessment like the one in Figure 1.2 can significantly benefit your instructional practices by helping you become more culturally responsive. Here's how that outcome can develop.

1. Increasing your cultural awareness

Efforts to increase your cultural awareness can begin with the following actions:

- **Understand your biases.** We all have biases, even if we don't always recognize them. Becoming aware of your cultural orientation—whether you lean more toward individualism or collectivism—helps you reflect on how these tendencies influence your expectations, communication, and classroom management.
- **Create a sense of belonging.** By understanding your own cultural orientation, you can better appreciate the diverse identities of your students. This awareness allows you to foster a classroom environment where every student feels accepted, supported, and included.

2. Adapting your teaching strategies

As you work to adapt your teaching strategies, you can take the following steps:

- **Tailor your instruction.** Although your standards and objectives should remain consistent, every class and grading period presents an opportunity to create unique learning experiences for your students. Knowing your own cultural orientation enables you to adjust your teaching methods to better meet the needs of students with different cultural values. For example, if you tend to prioritize independence,

you might intentionally incorporate more group work to support students who thrive on collaboration.
- **Balance activities.** Strive to provide a mix of individual and group activities to accommodate both individualistic and collectivist students. Balancing solo tasks with collaborative projects ensures that all students have opportunities to thrive in ways that align with their cultural preferences.

3. Engaging your students more effectively

Improved student engagement can result from prioritizing these two actions:

- **Make your content relatable.** Awareness of your cultural orientation—and how it may differ from your students'—helps you design lessons that are more engaging and relevant to their diverse backgrounds. This approach fosters a student-centered classroom that places their needs first. Although it's natural to teach based on your own preferences or how you were taught, offering choices between solo and group assignments ensures all students can engage meaningfully.
- **Communicate effectively.** Understanding your communication style, whether direct (common in individualistic cultures) or indirect (common in collectivist cultures), allows you to adapt your interactions to better connect with students who have different communication norms.

4. Forming stronger bonds with students

Strengthening bonds with students can be an attainable goal when you prioritize these behaviors:

- **Show empathy.** Self-awareness enhances your ability to empathize with students who experience the classroom

differently from you. This empathy can reduce frustration and improve your connection with students whose personalities or behaviors might initially seem challenging (think of Jason, for example).
- **Practice responsive classroom management.** By understanding both individualistic and collectivist needs, you can create a classroom community that nurtures all students. Creating this community leads to a more peaceful and effective learning environment.

5. Decreasing disproportionality

Keeping a balanced perspective regarding the individualist–collectivist spectrum is attainable when you do the following:

- **Make fair judgments.** Recognizing your cultural orientation helps you avoid making assumptions or judgments based on shared values—or differences—with your students. This mindset fosters fairness in grading, feedback, discipline, and overall opportunities for all students.
- **Practice culturally responsive teaching.** Teachers who are self-aware are more likely to adopt practices that value and honor students' cultural backgrounds. This approach can have an especially strong effect for students from collectivist cultures, providing them with the support they need to reach their full potential in environments that otherwise tend to tip toward individualism.

Individualistic Versus Collectivist Assignments

Classroom and homework assignments are foundational elements of teaching and learning, so it's essential to keep in mind how they relate to individualistic and collectivist cultural orientations.

Both the content and the methods for carrying out assignments are relevant. Let's take a closer look at the differences between individualistic and collectivist assignments.

Individualistic Assignments

Imagine you've given your students an assignment to write a personal essay about a significant achievement or accomplishment in their lives. You ask them to reflect on their experiences, share their story in detail, and highlight their personal effort and why the achievement matters to them. You provide grading criteria and a rubric that focuses on how well students articulate their personal journey, the challenges they faced, and the steps they took to overcome them.

This type of assignment is highly individualistic, emphasizing personal achievement and self-reliance. Students from individualistic cultures will likely thrive in this scenario. They are often accustomed to focusing on personal goals and accomplishments and may be engaged—or even excited—by the opportunity to share something meaningful about themselves with their teacher and classmates. However, this type of assignment can present challenges for students from collectivist backgrounds for several reasons, including the following:

- **Discomfort with self-promotion.** Students from collectivist backgrounds may not be used to talking about themselves or highlighting their achievements. They might feel uncomfortable or even perceive it as bragging to write extensively about their personal accomplishments.
- **Lack of familiarity with the format.** Collectivist students often view success as a group effort rather than an individual accomplishment. When asked to focus solely on their personal role, they may downplay their contributions or struggle to identify something they consider significant.

- **Potential for underperformance.** Because these students might feel hesitant or unsure about how to approach the task, their discomfort can negatively affect their performance. Ironically, an assignment meant to highlight their strengths could result in a poor grade simply because they struggle with the concept of self-promotion.

By understanding these challenges, educators can better support students from collectivist backgrounds in completing individualistic assignments.

> ### A Sidenote for Collectivist Teachers: The Elevator Pitch Activity
>
> In some of my professional development workshops, I used to conduct an activity called The Elevator Pitch. I'd ask the audience to imagine they are in an elevator on their way to a job interview. Dressed to impress, résumé in hand, they suddenly find themselves sharing the elevator with the CEO of the company they've dreamed of working for. They have just 60 seconds to make an impression. I would then ask for volunteers to "shoot their shot" by stepping forward and explaining, in 60 seconds or less, why the CEO should hire them.
>
> It was always fascinating to watch how people approached the task. Some participants would excel, confidently listing their years of experience, education, and volunteer work. They clearly articulated their value and why they were the perfect fit for the job.
>
> Others, however, struggled. They didn't know where to start, didn't want to come across as too assertive, or found it challenging to promote themselves—especially those from collectivist backgrounds, where humility and group success are often prioritized over self-promotion.
>
> How would you do in this activity?

Collectivist Assignments

Let's explore what a collectivist assignment might look like. For example, in a high school setting, students could be placed into small groups and tasked with addressing a current community issue, such as police oversight, housing access, or gentrification. Each group would research the topic, explore different perspectives, brainstorm possible solutions, and present their findings collaboratively.

In younger grades, collectivist projects might center around less emotionally charged topics that still hold real-world relevance. For instance, 4th or 5th graders might work in teams to investigate pollution associated with a nearby landfill or collaborate on how to preserve a local park or historic building scheduled for demolition. The focus in both cases remains the same: group interdependence, shared responsibility, and a common goal. These types of assignments provide space for students to contribute in ways that align with their strengths and cultural values.

The emphasis in this assignment is on teamwork, shared responsibility, and the group's ability to collaborate effectively. Each member plays a unique role, and the grading criteria include the following:

- How well the group works together.
- The quality of their collective output.
- How group members support one another throughout the process.

This type of assignment aligns with collectivist values by prioritizing group harmony, collaboration, and shared goals. Students from collectivist cultures are likely to thrive in this setting because it mirrors their cultural norm of working together toward a common purpose. However, students from individualistic backgrounds might encounter challenges in this type of assignment, including the following:

- **Struggles with group dynamics.** Students from individualistic backgrounds may find it difficult to share responsibility, especially if they are accustomed to being evaluated solely on their individual contributions.
- **Dominance or isolation.** An individualistic student might prefer to take charge of the project, doing most of the work themselves, or they might disengage entirely if they feel the group is not pulling its weight.
- **Perceived lack of effort.** If an individualistic student's participation style doesn't align with the group's approach, a teacher may misinterpret their behavior as uncooperative and possibly record a lower grade for their work compared to that of their peers.

These challenges highlight the importance of understanding and balancing cultural orientations within group activities to ensure fairness and engagement for all students.

The Impact of Cultural Norms on Classroom Behavior

The cultural norms of individualism and collectivism significantly shape how students engage in classroom activities. As we know, in the United States—a predominantly individualistic society—classroom structures often reflect a strong emphasis on independence and competition. For example, many classrooms are set up to promote individual work and self-reliance. It's not uncommon to see rows of individual desks where students sit in their own space, completing tasks independently (Tobia et al., 2022).

Silence, focus, and personal responsibility are prioritized, leaving little room for the type of group-oriented collaboration that aligns with collectivist values.

Even in classrooms with shared tables, the setup may not always support true interaction. Teachers might assign seating in ways that limit opportunities for movement or group engagement. For instance, students may remain in fixed seating arrangements, spending most of their time next to the same peers without the chance to work with others.

Classroom activities tilted toward either individualism or collectivism can unintentionally lead to misunderstandings about student behavior. Here are two examples:

- **Misinterpreting collectivist behavior.** Teachers unfamiliar with collectivist norms might view a student's desire to collaborate, even during tasks like silent reading or independent work, as disruptive or unfocused. In reality, this behavior reflects a cultural preference for shared learning and group engagement.
- **Misinterpreting individualistic behavior.** During collaborative activities, a student from an individualistic background might prefer to work alone or take on a leadership role, doing most of the work themselves. Teachers might interpret this as dominance or a lack of teamwork, when, in fact, the student is operating within the cultural framework they are accustomed to—one that values individual effort and leadership.

These misinterpretations can lead to unnecessary frustration for both teachers and students, underscoring the importance of designing classrooms and activities that consider cultural orientations.

Strategies for Culturally Responsive Teaching

Throughout this book, I'll provide strategies to help you recognize, assess, and adapt to your students' cultural dimensions to better meet their needs. You might be thinking, *No matter what I do, I'm going to favor one way or the other, and someone will be left out.* By the end of this book, however, you'll know how to tap into the greatness each student brings to the table and show them they are valued members of your classroom community.

Creating a stronger sense of belonging starts with awareness of cultural dimensions and a willingness to adjust your teaching practices. I especially encourage my veteran teachers—those who've been teaching the same lessons, giving the same assessments, and structuring their classrooms the same way for years—to take a step back and reflect. What areas in your practice might need tweaking to ensure you're fostering a well-rounded, inclusive environment? Here are four strategies you can implement right away:

1. **Balance individual and group work.**
   - Review your current unit and lesson plans.
   - Create a list of the assessments you plan to assign, and count how many are individualistic versus collectivist.
   - Make changes to ensure your curriculum includes a mix of assignments catering to both cultural preferences. For example, pair personal essays with group projects to give all students opportunities to shine in different contexts. This approach not only promotes fairness but also encourages students to develop skills in both individual and group settings.

2. **Intentionally teach collaboration skills.**
   - Build in scaffolding time to teach students how to work in groups effectively.
   - Provide explicit instruction on essential skills such as active listening, compromise, and shared decision making.
   - Offer practice opportunities so students—particularly those more accustomed to individual work—can develop these abilities, which are essential not only in school but also in their future roles as adults. By teaching collaboration skills now, you're giving your students a head start.
3. **Create culturally sensitive assessments.**
   - When designing tests and quizzes, consider both group performance and individual contributions, ensuring that students from both individualistic and collectivist backgrounds feel fairly evaluated. For example, pair group projects where students can demonstrate teamwork and shared accountability with individual evaluations.
4. **Encourage reflection on cultural norms.**
   - Teach your students about individualism and collectivism, and encourage them to reflect on their own cultural backgrounds and how these influence their learning preferences.
   - Facilitate classroom discussions where students share their perspectives and learn from each other.
   - Create reflective writing assignments that help students explore their cultural values and how those values shape their behaviors and attitudes.

These four strategies foster empathy, self-awareness, and mutual understanding among your students.

Summing Up and Looking Ahead

Just as the way you manage your refrigerator may reflect your cultural values (as I noted at the start of this chapter), the way you design your classrooms and interact with students significantly affects their learning experiences. Recognizing and integrating the cultural dimensions of individualism and collectivism into your teaching practices can create a stronger sense of belonging and a more supportive learning environment. By balancing individual and group activities, teaching with cultural sensitivity, and acknowledging the diverse backgrounds of your students, you can help every student feel valued and capable of succeeding in your classroom.

In the next chapter, I encourage you to reconsider your approach to classroom management. Too often, the term *classroom management* focuses on control and compliance. Many traditional teaching strategies emphasize quiet, orderly classrooms, suppressing collaboration and individual expression. Unfortunately, these approaches often lack cultural sensitivity and fail to meet the needs of all students. Let's explore how rethinking classroom management can lead to more inclusive, engaging, and culturally responsive environments.

2

Rethinking Classroom Management

Classroom management is one of the foundational components of teacher preparation programs. Alongside lesson planning, differentiation, and instructional strategies, new teachers are taught a range of methods to create and maintain an orderly learning environment.

I'm not a fan of the term *classroom management* on its own. It's outdated, heavily emphasizes control and compliance, and places too much focus on rigid behavioral standards. The phrase itself isn't student-centered, and its connotation often reflects authoritarian practices that leave little room for student autonomy.

Some might argue that this is merely semantics or the fault of educators who lean too heavily on controlling behaviors rather than creating opportunities for students to self-regulate and thrive. Alfie Kohn (2021) asserts that much of the focus has been on controlling students rather than consulting with them, supporting them, or building meaningful relationships.

The reality is that these "traditional" practices often reflect mainstream, individualistic cultural norms that don't align with today's multicultural classrooms or account for the diverse cultural values of students who bring unique experiences and perspectives to the classroom. It's time to shift the emphasis to constructing caring classroom communities where teachers actively listen to students—both as individuals and as members of a collective. It's clear that a rethinking of classroom management is overdue.

Research has shown that seating arrangements play a significant role in student achievement and engagement (Cheryan et al., 2014; Price & Pace, 2005). Walk into most classrooms in the United States and you're likely to see desks arranged in rows, promoting a teacher-centered environment where students work independently (Tobia et al., 2022). This traditional setup often includes the teacher's desk prominently placed at the front of the room, reinforcing a hierarchical dynamic.

Even in classrooms with tables and chairs, students are often expected to conform to the teacher's behavioral expectations, which may restrict their ability to express themselves authentically. Some students adapt to these norms, becoming what the teacher considers an "ideal student," whereas others feel safe to be themselves only outside the classroom—or even off school grounds.

Alternatively, student-centered seating arrangements, such as clusters or group tables, encourage collaboration and peer interaction (Tobia et al., 2022). Teachers generally prefer these layouts, as they foster a sense of community and make group work more natural (Gremmen et al., 2016).

This chapter challenges you to critically examine your current classroom management practices, particularly your physical space, and consider whether they prioritize student engagement, expression, and belonging, or whether they enforce narrow behavioral standards that suppress students' cultural identities. Additionally, this chapter will guide you through strategies to move beyond traditional classroom management and toward meaningful practices that foster inclusion, belonging, and authentic student engagement. By enhancing your Teacher VIBE (Valuing Inclusion and Belonging for Everyone), you can create a classroom that supports both individual and collective needs.

Classroom Management and Its Pitfalls

The term *classroom management* is widely used to describe the processes and strategies teachers employ to maintain order, promote learning, and address behavioral issues (Wolff et al., 2021). However, this concept has faced increasing criticism for failing to meet the needs of culturally diverse classrooms, particularly in the post-COVID era (Gülmez & Ordu, 2022; Kohn, 2021).

If we're not careful, traditional classroom management approaches can result in the following pitfalls:

- **Control over connection.** The teacher–student dynamic prioritizes control over building positive relationships and a supportive classroom community.
- **Compliance over autonomy.** Teachers focus on order and obedience, leaving little room for students to develop self-regulation, decision-making skills, and ownership of their learning process.
- **Marginalization of certain groups.** A one-size-fits-all approach may unintentionally exclude students from diverse cultural backgrounds whose behaviors or values differ from mainstream norms.

- **Reactive rather than proactive action.** Instead of proactively creating environments that encourage engagement and positive behaviors, teachers address issues only as they arise.
- **Missed opportunities for collaboration.** The lack of cooperative learning and peer support stifles students' ability to develop meaningful relationships and teamwork skills.
- **Absence of modeling.** Teachers may fail to demonstrate the importance of collaboration, leaving students unprepared for group-oriented tasks in the future.

The Teacher VIBE: Balancing Individualistic and Collectivist Cultural Norms in the Classroom

In Chapter 1, I introduced you to Hofstede's cultural dimensions theory and the concept of individualistic versus collectivist cultural norms. If you completed the Self-Assessment for Cultural Awareness (Figure 1.2), you've already explored whether you lean more toward individualism or collectivism.

We've discussed the importance of balancing your teaching practices to meet the diverse needs of students, each of whom brings unique values, perspectives, and experiences to the classroom. Whereas some students may come from individualistic cultures that emphasize personal achievement and independence, others may come from collectivist cultures that prioritize community, cooperation, and shared success.

My challenge to you is to be intentional about creating a classroom environment that respects and supports both mindsets. That's where the Teacher VIBE comes in.

What Is the Teacher VIBE?

The Teacher VIBE is a mindset: Valuing Inclusion and Belonging for Everyone. It's about ensuring that all students—whether they thrive on individual achievement or group collaboration—feel accepted, supported, and included in your classroom. Let's break down the acronym.

Valuing: Recognizing the unique characteristics of each student as priceless attributes in your classroom environment

Valuing students means creating a balance between individualistic and collectivist cultural norms. This balance includes celebrating personal achievements while also recognizing how individuals contribute to the group. You can achieve this balance by taking the following actions:

- **For individualistic students**, acknowledge and celebrate individual achievements and leadership.
- **For collectivist students**, provide opportunities for group success, collaboration, and teamwork.

What could this look like?

- Offering personalized affirmations for individual successes, whether academic or personal
- Planning collaborative activities and affirming how students contribute to team goals
- Allowing students to showcase their unique talents, either individually or as part of a group

Inclusion: Ensuring every student has a seat at the table in both individual and collective contexts

Inclusion means fostering buy-in from students of all backgrounds, inviting them to play an active role in classroom activities. Whether students excel in independent tasks or group settings, inclusion ensures they feel valued and engaged. You can foster inclusion by taking the following actions:

- **For individualistic students**, provide opportunities for self-expression and independent work that highlights their strengths.
- **For collectivist students**, encourage group-based activities that emphasize collaboration and mutual support.

What could this look like?

- Involving students in co-creating projects and activities based on their preferences
- Incorporating content and activities that reflect students' lived experiences and interests
- Encouraging peer support and mentorship to bridge individual and collective contributions

Belonging: Ensuring each student feels welcomed and recognized as an essential member of the classroom

Belonging is universal, but it manifests differently across cultural norms. Students from individualistic backgrounds often feel belonging through recognition of their individuality, whereas collectivist students may find belonging in their contributions to the group. You can create a sense of belonging by taking the following actions:

- **For individualistic students**, celebrate their identity and unique role in the classroom.
- **For collectivist students**, foster a sense of community and connection to a larger, supportive group.

What could this look like?

- Creating opportunities for students to share personal stories and celebrating their accomplishments

- Establishing classroom traditions or rituals that build a sense of group identity and unity
- Ensuring every student has a voice through individual presentations and group discussions

Everyone: Taking intentional steps to build strong teacher–student and student–student bonds

The key to the Teacher VIBE is understanding that *everyone* deserves to feel valued. By respecting both individual achievements and collective success, you create a classroom culture that honors diversity and builds meaningful connections. You can affirm that everyone has value by taking the following actions:

- **For individualistic students**, offer individualized feedback, goal setting, and leadership opportunities.
- **For collectivist students**, create group-based learning goals, collaborative assignments, and opportunities for teamwork.

What could this look like?

- Establishing flexible classroom dynamics where students can lead independently or contribute collaboratively based on their strengths
- Modeling respect for differences among students and affirming that every student is worthy of love and appreciation
- Exploring students' cultural preferences together, encouraging them to value their peers and appreciate the importance of both individualistic and collectivist cultural norms

Why the Teacher VIBE Matters

Balancing individualistic and collectivist cultural norms through the Teacher VIBE ensures that all students feel valued, supported, and included. It's a mindset that fosters understanding, builds empathy, and strengthens the sense of belonging within your classroom. By intentionally valuing inclusion and belonging for everyone, you create a learning environment where every student can thrive, whether as an independent leader or a vital team player.

Balancing Individualistic and Collectivist Values with the Teacher VIBE

The Teacher VIBE is not a framework; it's a mindset. It's about intentionally cultivating a classroom environment that does the following:

- **Respects and celebrates individual achievements.** Recognize and support students who thrive by showcasing their unique skills, talents, and ideas.
- **Advocates for collective responsibility and student buy-in.** Collaborate with your students to create experiences that harness teamwork, cooperation, and shared goals.
- **Encourages cross-cultural understanding.** Teach students about their own cultural norms while modeling how to honor, appreciate, and learn from others' values.

Key Benefits of the Teacher VIBE

Adopting the Teacher VIBE mindset is well worth the effort. Here are three key benefits of doing so:

- **Increased student engagement.** Students from both individualistic and collectivist backgrounds feel accepted, supported, and included, leading to higher levels of engagement.

- **Enhanced classroom harmony.** Balancing personal and group success fosters respect and unity across cultural norms.
- **Deeper learning experiences.** Students grow not only academically but also socially and emotionally as they learn to appreciate diverse perspectives.

Practical Strategies for Balancing the VIBE

In the previous sections, I've offered suggestions for how to develop the VIBE mindset. Here are some overarching strategies for ensuring a balance between collectivist and individualistic cultural norms in the classroom:

- **Offer a mix of individual and collaborative activities.** Take a student-centered approach by inviting students to help design learning opportunities. Let them choose how they engage with tasks. Some may prefer to work independently, whereas others will excel in group settings.
- **Celebrate both individual and group accomplishments.** Recognize all forms of success, whether it's a student's personal academic achievement or a team's collaborative effort. This all-encompassing recognition ensures every type of contribution is valued.
- **Create spaces for self-expression and collective input.** Use classroom tools such as sharing circles, classroom discussions, or bulletin boards to give students opportunities to express themselves individually and as part of a group.
- **Advocate for collaboration across cultural boundaries.** Pair or group students from different cultural backgrounds to encourage mutual learning, understanding, and empathy.

The Teacher VIBE means honoring both individual achievement and collective growth. It requires teachers to respect and integrate the different cultural values that students bring into the classroom, creating a space where everyone feels accepted, supported, and included.

VIBE Check: Is My Classroom Collectivist Friendly?

I want you to take some time to consider your classroom environment. Students should walk into your classroom feeling like a valued member of your classroom community, seeing it as a place where every student feels accepted, supported, and included. Considering all the challenges a student may face outside school, the classroom should be a place that welcomes people of all identities and cultural backgrounds.

The self-assessment in Figure 2.1 is intended to prompt reflection on how well your classroom supports collectivist cultural norms, which are often essential characteristics related to students' identities and experiences. Use it to honestly evaluate your current facilitation, instructional practices, and culturally responsive practices and identify areas for growth. Remember, the goal is continuous growth and progress toward creating a classroom where all students, with their multiple identities, are truly valued.

Completing the self-assessment in Figure 2.1 is a significant step in your journey to creating a classroom environment that supports the diverse cultural norms of your students. Your classroom can become a space that honors both individualistic and collectivist values, maintaining a balance between dignity and freedom.

FIGURE 2.1
Self-Assessment for Classroom Environment

Instructions
For each question, circle the response that best describes your practice.

Section 1: Classroom Environment and Physical Setup

1. **Seating Arrangements**
   Do you regularly arrange desks in clusters or circles to facilitate group work and discussion?
   - Always
   - Often
   - Sometimes
   - Rarely
   - Never

2. **Collaboration Zones**
   Does your classroom have designated areas where students can work together on projects or engage in group activities?
   - Always
   - Often
   - Sometimes
   - Rarely
   - Never

3. **Flexible Seating**
   Do you offer flexible seating options that allow students to choose where they sit based on their learning preferences?
   - Always
   - Often
   - Sometimes
   - Rarely
   - Never

4. **Visual Representation of Cultural Diversity**
   Are diverse cultures represented in your classroom through posters, decorations, and learning materials?
   - Always
   - Often
   - Sometimes
   - Rarely
   - Never

Section 2: Classroom Management and Behavioral Expectations

5. **Collaborative Rulemaking**
   Do you involve students in the creation of classroom rules and expectations?
   - Always
   - Often
   - Sometimes
   - Rarely
   - Never

6. **Cultural Sensitivity in Rules**
   Are your classroom rules and expectations designed to reflect and respect the cultural norms of all students?
   — Always
   — Often
   — Sometimes
   — Rarely
   — Never

7. **Conflict Resolution**
   Do you use restorative practices (e.g., circle processes, restorative conversations) to address conflicts in your classroom?
   — Always
   — Often
   — Sometimes
   — Rarely
   — Never

8. **Emphasis on Group Harmony**
   Do your classroom management practices emphasize group harmony and collective responsibility over individual achievement?
   — Always
   — Often
   — Sometimes
   — Rarely
   — Never

Section 3: Instructional Practices

9. **Group Work and Cooperative Learning**
   How frequently do you incorporate group work and cooperative learning activities into your lessons?
   — Always
   — Often
   — Sometimes
   — Rarely
   — Never

10. **Cultural Relevance in Curriculum**
    Do you integrate culturally relevant content and perspectives into your curriculum?
    — Always
    — Often
    — Sometimes
    — Rarely
    — Never

(continued)

FIGURE 2.1
Self-Assessment for Classroom Environment (*Continued*)

11. Recognition of Collective Effort
Do you recognize and reward collective effort and group achievements as much as individual accomplishments?
— Always
— Often
— Sometimes
— Rarely
— Never

12. Peer Learning Opportunities
Do you create opportunities for peer teaching and learning where students can share their knowledge and skills with one another?
— Always
— Often
— Sometimes
— Rarely
— Never

Section 4: Teacher–Student Relationships

13. Understanding Cultural Backgrounds
Do you take time to learn about the cultural backgrounds of your students and use that knowledge to inform your teaching?
— Always
— Often
— Sometimes
— Rarely
— Never

14. Building Community
Do you actively work to build a sense of community and belonging in your classroom, where all students feel accepted, supported, and included?
— Always
— Often
— Sometimes
— Rarely
— Never

15. Culturally Responsive Communication
Do you adapt your communication style to be more culturally responsive to the needs of your students?
— Always
— Often
— Sometimes
— Rarely
— Never

Scoring and Reflection
- **Score 4 points** for each "Always" response.
- **Score 3 points** for each "Often" response.
- **Score 2 points** for each "Sometimes" response.
- **Score 1 point** for each "Rarely" response.
- **Score 0 points** for each "Never" response.

Total Possible Points: 60

Interpretation of Scores
50–60 points: It is evident that you are deeply committed to collectivist cultural norms. This mindset creates an environment where collaboration, cultural understanding, and a strong sense of community are highly valued.
35–49 points: Your classroom has strong collectivist practices, but there are still opportunities for growth in meeting the needs of all students.
20–34 points: Your classroom management and instructional practices might be more effective with a stronger emphasis on collectivist cultural norms. Consider starting the work now and tapping into the strategies and resources in this book.
Below 20 points: There is a lot of room for growth in supporting the needs of your collectivist students. Reflect on areas where you might be unintentionally marginalizing certain students, and think about what actions would help create more balance in your practices.

Once you have your results, consider focusing on one or two areas where you scored lower than desired. Create a game plan to address those areas, using one or more of the following suggestions:

- Rearrange your classroom layout to promote more group work.
- Incorporate literature that reflects the cultures of your students.
- Implement community-building circles or restorative practices.

These adjustments, though seemingly small, can make a significant difference in fostering an environment where everyone feels welcome, valued, and supported. Remember, this is a journey, not a destination. Growth takes time, reflection, and intentional action.

From Control to Community: Embracing Restorative Practices in School

To create a learning environment where all students feel accepted and included, teachers must rethink traditional classroom management approaches (Darling-Hammond & Fronius, 2023). This shift requires unlearning outdated methods and embracing a model that values grace, respect, and cultural responsiveness.

Let's keep it real—no classroom is perfect. We're working with adolescents, after all, and challenges will arise. Although taking steps to maintain order is necessary at times, we can reduce many challenges by proactively building relationships and addressing behaviors in ways that teach responsibility and empathy. Achieving this goal is why I advocate for incorporating *restorative practices* into your Teacher VIBE.

Restorative Practices: A Great Tool to Add to Your Teacher VIBE Bag

Restorative practices focus on repairing harm, restoring relationships, and fostering a sense of belonging. Instead of exclusionary actions like suspensions or expulsions, these practices address the root causes of conflict and resolve them through dialogue and mutual understanding (Darling-Hammond, 2023).

The benefits of restorative practices include the following:

- Promoting positive relationships between peers and between students and teachers (Lodi et al., 2021).

- Building safer, more positive learning communities (Zakszeski & Rutherford, 2021).
- Reducing overall rates of conflicts and misbehavior (Darling-Hammond & Fronius, 2023).
- Supporting a strong sense of belonging (Lodi et al., 2021).

Restorative practices are an essential addition to your Teacher VIBE toolkit. The following are some examples of these practices in action.

Restorative circles

Restorative circles provide students with a platform to share emotions, build deeper connections with peers, and resolve conflicts positively through community support (Darling-Hammond, 2023). Consider starting your day or class with a circle to check in on your students. For example, you might ask, "What are you looking forward to this weekend?" Students can share their thoughts or pass if they prefer. Circles can also be used for classroom discussions, collaborative decision making, or conflict resolution (Zakszeski & Rutherford, 2021). In a circle, every student has an equal voice, aligning with the values of collectivist cultures, which prioritize group harmony and mutual respect.

Restorative conversations

When conflicts arise, restorative conversations encourage students to reflect on their behavior, understand its impact, and collaboratively find solutions (Darling-Hammond, 2023). For instance, when addressing a conflict, invite all involved parties to share their perspectives. Ask reflective questions such as these:

- "What were you thinking when this happened?"
- "How do you think the other person felt at that moment?"

This approach repairs relationships, fosters accountability, and strengthens community bonds. It moves away from punitive measures that avoid addressing the conflict and instead focuses on meaningful resolutions (Darling-Hammond & Fronius, 2023).

Moving Forward

Restorative practices are just one component of creating a culturally responsive and inclusive classroom environment. By integrating these tools into your Teacher VIBE, you'll foster stronger relationships, reduce conflicts, and cultivate a sense of belonging for all students.

As you continue on this journey, remember that small, intentional changes can lead to significant impacts over time. Let your Teacher VIBE guide you in creating a classroom that balances individual and collective values, embraces diversity, and supports every student's success.

Building a Student-Centered Classroom Community Agreement

One of the best ways to align your classroom with the cultural norms of your students is by involving them in creating classroom community agreements—rules and protocols that guide behavior and expectations. Although this effort might seem like a no-brainer, it's an opportunity that's often overlooked in classrooms.

Inviting students to actively participate in setting expectations fosters ownership and buy-in. It allows students to feel like integral members of the classroom, shaping how it operates. Moreover, this approach ensures that the classroom agreements reflect the values, experiences, and needs of everyone, rather than imposing a one-size-fits-all model.

Creating Student-Centered Protocols

At the start of the year, engage your students in a discussion about the behaviors and expectations that foster a positive learning environment. Ask them what they expect from you as their teacher and what they believe is essential for creating a respectful and supportive classroom community. Encourage them to bring their cultural perspectives into the conversation. Together, you can build a meaningful classroom community agreement that feels inclusive and empowering.

Here are some specific steps to take as you and your students create a classroom community agreement:

1. **Set the stage.** Begin by explaining to your students that you value each of them and want to create the agreement as a team. Share that the purpose of the agreement is to establish protocols for how everyone will work together, show respect, and maintain a positive learning space. Emphasize that this classroom is as much theirs as it is yours, and their input is essential.
2. **Initiate dialogue.** Start with open-ended questions that encourage students to share their thoughts on the ideal classroom environment. To ensure everyone feels comfortable participating, offer options for students to respond anonymously on paper. This approach respects both individualistic and collectivist norms. Here are examples of questions to ask:
    - What types of behaviors create a positive learning space?
    - What expectations do you have of me as your teacher?
    - How should we treat each other as classmates?
    - What actions make you feel valued and appreciated?

3. **Brainstorm ideas.** As students share their ideas, take notes (or ask a student to do so) to document their input. To encourage participation and gather diverse perspectives, consider pairing students or dividing them into small groups for discussion. Afterward, identify common themes such as respect, accountability, and communication.
4. **Create a draft together.** Using the shared ideas and themes, collaborate with your class to draft the community agreement. Ensure the language is clear, age-appropriate, and relatable for your students. The agreement should balance individualistic values, like personal responsibility, with collectivist values, like group harmony and teamwork.
5. **Review and revise.** Distribute the draft to your students and invite feedback. Ask if there's anything missing or if adjustments need to be made. Go through the suggestions as a class and revise the agreement together, ensuring everyone feels heard and represented.
6. **Finalize and post the agreement.** Once the agreement is finalized, post it prominently in your classroom as a visible reminder of your shared commitment. Refer to it as needed throughout the year, reminding students of their role in upholding the agreement—and inviting them to remind you if necessary.
7. **Revisit and adjust.** Periodically revisit the agreement, especially after significant conflicts or incidents. Use these moments to reflect on whether the agreement is still meeting the needs of the classroom. If adjustments are necessary, make revisions together. If not, take the opportunity to reaffirm everyone's commitment.

Why This Approach Matters

By involving students in the creation of classroom community agreements, you're not only setting expectations but also building a foundation of trust, respect, and inclusivity. This collaborative process helps students feel valued and invested in their learning environment, making it easier to balance individualistic and collectivist cultural norms.

When students see themselves as active participants in shaping their classroom experience, they are more likely to take ownership of their behavior and contribute to a positive, supportive community. See Figure 2.2 for a sample classroom community agreement.

Making It Memorable

The sample agreement in Figure 2.2 reflects a balance of individualistic and collectivist values. To make it easier for students to remember, consider creating an acronym together as a class. Here are some examples:

- **RESPECT:** Responsibility, Empathy, Support, Positivity, Equity, Communication, Teamwork
- **CARES:** Collaboration, Accountability, Respect, Empathy, Safety
- **PRIDE:** Positivity, Responsibility, Inclusion, Diversity, Excellence
- **SHARE:** Support, Harmony, Accountability, Respect, Engagement
- **TEAM:** Together Everyone Achieves More
- **GROWTH:** Gratitude, Respect, Openness, Well-being, Trust, Harmony

FIGURE 2.2
Sample Classroom Community Agreement

Our Classroom Values and Expectations

1. Respect for Everyone's Voice
We will listen to one another with open minds and value each person's opinions, even when they differ from our own.

2. Support for Teamwork
We will work together as a team, supporting each other in our learning. If someone is struggling, we will offer help. When someone succeeds, we will celebrate their achievements.

3. Our Responsibility
Each of us will take responsibility for our own actions and learning. We will come to class prepared, complete our work on time, and contribute to maintaining a positive learning environment.

4. Appreciating Differences
We will honor and value the unique differences and experiences of everyone in our classroom. We will be mindful of how our words and actions affect others, ensuring that everyone feels accepted, supported, and included.

5. Open Communication
We will communicate openly and honestly. When challenges or disagreements arise, we will work together to resolve them with kindness and respect, ensuring that everyone's perspective is heard and considered.

6. Positive and Brave Learning Space
We will create and maintain a safe and supportive environment that encourages everyone to take risks in their learning. Mistakes will be viewed as opportunities for growth.

7. Mutual Respect for Boundaries
We will respect each other's personal, physical, and emotional boundaries, ensuring everyone feels secure and comfortable in our classroom. This respect includes being mindful of cultural differences in personal space and communication styles.

8. Everyone's Classroom
We will take care of our classroom together by keeping it clean and organized. We will respect shared materials and spaces, recognizing that this is our collective learning home.

Our Agreement in Action
- We will regularly revisit and reflect on our community agreement to ensure it continues to meet everyone's needs.
- If changes are necessary, we will discuss them as a group and adjust together.

Collaborating on creating an acronym can be a fun and engaging way to reinforce the values in your classroom community agreement.

Seating Arrangements to Balance Individualistic and Collectivist Needs

The physical layout of your classroom significantly affects your students' sense of belonging and reflects your Teacher VIBE. By thoughtfully arranging the space, you can create areas that support both team players and solo stars. Figure 2.3 lists various options for seating arrangements, which can foster collaboration, independence, and a sense of community while considering the

FIGURE 2.3
Classroom Seating Arrangements

Seating Arrangement	Purpose	Visual
Perimeter clusters	Collectivist interaction	
Dual-purpose desks	Balance between independent and collaborative work	
Independent desk area	Individualistic focus	
Rotational seating	Flexibility	
Collaborative zones	Teamwork	
Personalized learning corners	Personal reflection or independent study	
U-shaped seating	Maximizing eye contact and attention	

diverse cultural backgrounds of your students. Here is a more detailed look at these options:

- **Perimeter clusters (for encouraging collectivist interaction)**
  — **Description:** Desks are arranged in clusters of two to six students, promoting discussions, cooperation, and teamwork.
  — **Implementation:** Distribute clusters around the classroom perimeter, ensuring clear boundaries between groups for personal space. Offer a mix of smaller and larger clusters.
  — **Purpose:** Students from collectivist cultures benefit from collaborative spaces, whereas those from individualistic cultures can opt for controlled involvement (Bluteau et al., 2022).
- **Dual-purpose desks (for balancing independence and collaboration)**
  — **Description:** Pairs of desks are spaced slightly apart from larger clusters and can be used for independent work or quick collaboration.
  — **Implementation:** Place paired desks in the classroom's center or front to provide a balance of independence and accessibility.
  — **Purpose:** This setup supports both individual focus and the possibility of one-on-one collaboration (Salma & Şahin, 2022).
- **Independent desk area (for supporting individualistic focus)**
  — **Description:** A section of the classroom has single desks that are spaced apart for students who prefer working alone.

- **Implementation:** Position the desks along the back or side walls to create a quieter, distraction-free zone.
- **Purpose:** This option is ideal for students from individualistic cultures seeking personal space, creativity, and concentration, while also offering a retreat for collectivist students when needed (Tobia et al., 2022).

• **Rotational seating (for fostering flexibility)**
- **Description:** Seating arrangements are rotated periodically to give students experience in both independent and collaborative environments.
- **Implementation:** Change seating every few weeks, quarter, or semester, alternating students between clusters, pairs, and independent desks.
- **Purpose:** This option encourages collectivist students to develop independent skills and individualistic students to build teamwork abilities (German et al., 2020).

• **Collaborative zones (for encouraging teamwork)**
- **Description:** Round tables, semicircular seating, or open floor spaces are dedicated for work on group projects.
- **Implementation:** Position these zones near the center of the classroom or the whiteboard to encourage interaction during collaborative activities.
- **Purpose:** Designed for collectivist cultures that value group harmony, these zones provide opportunities for teamwork and collective problem solving (Yang et al., 2021).

- **Personalized learning corners (for fostering reflection and independence)**
    - **Description:** Quiet, semi-private spaces are furnished with comfortable seating, like beanbags or armchairs, for independent study or reflection.
    - **Implementation:** Locate one or two corners in the back or side of the room, away from high-traffic areas.
    - **Purpose:** These areas cater to individualistic students who prefer introspective, autonomous work while offering a calming retreat for any student needing focus or quiet (Nehyba et al., 2021).
- **U-shaped seating (for maximizing whole-class engagement)**
    - **Description:** Desks are arranged in a U-shape or horseshoe pattern, with the open end facing the teacher. All students can see and interact with each other.
    - **Implementation:** Arrange desks in a U-shape around the classroom's teaching area, leaving ample space between desks for personal comfort.
    - **Purpose:** This layout promotes open discussions and collaboration, which aligns with collectivist values, while maintaining individual space for students from individualistic backgrounds (Syaifullah et al., 2022).

Why Consider Flexible Seating?

Allowing students to choose their seats from a variety of options fosters a sense of ownership and autonomy. If you typically assign name tags to desks, consider letting students choose their seats first and then place their name tags accordingly.

Flexible seating also limits biases in seat assignments, creating a more inclusive atmosphere, where students feel a stronger sense of community.

Key Takeaways

Your classroom layout should reflect your Teacher VIBE, balancing the needs of individualistic and collectivist students. As you think about how to arrange your classroom, keep these suggestions in mind:

- Incorporate spaces for collaboration and teamwork alongside areas for focused, independent work.
- Regularly assess your seating arrangement to ensure it meets the cultural and academic needs of your students.
- Encourage student ownership by involving them in decisions about where and how they learn best.

By intentionally designing your classroom to respect cultural diversity, you create an environment where team players and solo stars alike can thrive.

The Need for a Shift

As Tomlinson (2023) aptly states, "Learning requires structure and order, but the structure and order should be in service of learning—not for the sake of demonstrating who's in charge." This sentiment perfectly encapsulates why I'm not a fan of the term *classroom management* on its own. Too often it emphasizes compliance and control rather than fostering a sense of community where students feel valued and supported.

A classroom should be a *student-centered community* where learning thrives and every student feels they belong. Rethinking traditional classroom management means being open to other ways of connecting with students and creating an environment that respects their diverse cultural norms and learning preferences.

The Teacher VIBE—Valuing Inclusion and Belonging for Everyone—is a mindset to guide this shift. It's about ensuring that every student feels accepted, supported, and included within the learning community. This goal involves balancing the needs of individualistic students who excel in independent work with the needs of collectivist students who thrive in collaborative settings. It's about creating spaces where all students can both shine individually and contribute meaningfully to a group.

Summing Up and Looking Ahead

In this chapter, I shared practical steps for rethinking classroom dynamics around three main elements:

- **Recognizing and celebrating different kinds of achievements**, honoring both personal milestones and collective successes.
- **Involving students in creating classroom community agreements**, ensuring they have ownership of the rules and protocols that guide their shared space.
- **Designing seating arrangements that promote both individual tasks and group collaboration**, allowing for flexibility and student choice.

These strategies may seem simple, but they can have a profound effect on how students engage in the classroom and how they see themselves within the learning environment.

In Chapter 3, we'll build upon the Teacher VIBE with the Teacher LENS framework. The chapter will equip you with tools to observe, analyze, and interpret student behaviors and nonverbal cues through a cultural lens. By sharpening your observational skills and examining your own cultural biases, you'll gain deeper insights into how these biases influence your perceptions of students. Detailed examples will illustrate how these skills can uncover behaviors rooted in collectivist values, like teamwork and cooperation, helping you further refine your teaching practices to support a diverse classroom community.

3

Mastering Classroom Observations with the Teacher LENS

When I first began teaching, my classroom often felt like a never-ending game of Red Light, Green Light. Despite all the pedagogical theories and strategies I had learned in my teacher preparation program, nothing could have prepared me for teaching overseas in the U.S. Virgin Islands. I was ambitious and eager to make a difference in this new environment, yet I lacked an understanding of the culture I was serving and the deep history of the locals.

I approached classroom management by setting clear "red lights" and "green lights" for my students. "Red light" meant silence during independent work, eyes on their papers, and hands to themselves. "Green light" meant raising hands to speak and working quietly at their desks. To me, these rules were essential for maintaining order and focus, just as I had been taught.

However, my students didn't always respond to these traditional classroom management practices. During "red light" times, my students talked, collaborated, and even walked around to help one another. I grew frustrated, wondering why they were ignoring my clear directions. I began marking them down for what I saw as disruptive behavior, thinking I was doing the right thing. It didn't occur to me that I was grading their behavior instead of their understanding of the material.

As the semester progressed, the classroom atmosphere became tense, and some students disengaged. I clung to my rules, convinced that enforcing compliance would eventually bring order. But the reality was, I was playing Red Light, Green Light based on a different set of rules than those my students were familiar with.

The breakthrough came during a parent-teacher conference. The mother of one of my students asked where I was from, noting my accent and politely remarking that I didn't seem like an "island boy." After I explained that I was from Texas, she gently clarified something I had missed: In their community culture, talking through problems and working together wasn't a sign of disrespect; it was a way of showing engagement and support. Verbal processing and group collaboration were how her child, and many others in the community, learned best.

That conversation was my light-bulb moment. My rigid "red lights" were stifling my students' natural ways of learning. Their behavior wasn't defiance; it was an expression of cultural norms that I hadn't taken the time to understand. I had been so focused on enforcing my rules that I failed to see how they clashed with my students' values and culture styles.

The following week, I approached my classroom differently. Instead of demanding silence and independent work, I started creating opportunities for collaboration and verbal processing. I encouraged group discussions, allowed students to move around and help one another, and embraced their way of learning.

The change was remarkable. My students were suddenly more engaged, energized, and connected to the material. By adjusting my approach—offering new "green lights" where I once had enforced "red lights"—I learned to respect and embrace their cultural norms. This shift taught me that success in the classroom isn't about enforcing the rules I believe are right but about *understanding when to stop and when to go* based on the community I'm serving.

The moral of this story is that we educators must be willing to adapt our expectations and practices to align with the cultural contexts of our students. Much like in the game Red Light, Green Light, where success depends on recognizing when to move or stop based on external signals, teaching requires us to recognize when our "red lights" may unnecessarily hinder culturally appropriate behaviors.

This chapter will teach you to use your Teacher LENS to observe your students' behaviors and identify potential mismatches between your expectations and their cultural norms. The Teacher LENS framework aligns with the Teacher VIBE (Valuing Inclusion and Belonging for Everyone) mindset described in Chapter 2, emphasizing careful observation of how students communicate, collaborate, and engage in your classroom.

Specifically, you'll learn (1) how to use the Teacher LENS to analyze and interpret student behaviors through a cultural lens; (2) strategies for active listening, fly-on-the-wall observations, and interpreting nonverbal cues to better understand your students; (3) ways to reduce unintentional misunderstandings and discipline issues stemming from cultural differences; and (4) how cultural awareness in observation can transform classroom dynamics. By the time you reach the end of this chapter, you'll feel confident in your ability to observe with cultural context, minimize misunderstandings, and create a classroom where every student feels seen, valued, and supported.

Seeing Beneath the Surface: Rethinking Student Observation Practices

As you've read the previous chapters, you've done a lot of self-reflection and assessment. Now it's time to examine your student observation practices. As caring teachers, we often observe our students' behaviors to understand their emotional states, focus levels, interactions, and engagement. However, as human beings, we bring our own set of cultural expectations and biases into the classroom, often without realizing it (Eakins, 2022).

Most teachers in the United States, for example, come from individualistic cultural backgrounds that celebrate values like independence, self-reliance, and competition. These traditional approaches to teaching and learning influence how we view behaviors in the classroom. Actions like working independently, maintaining silence, and following strict rules may be seen as markers of a "good" student.

However, for students from collectivist cultures, which emphasize collaboration, verbal processing, and collective success, such behaviors might conflict with how they naturally engage with and process information. For instance, a student speaking during an independent task might be seen as disruptive when, in fact, they are engaging in verbal processing, which is a common and culturally appropriate learning strategy in many societies.

As educators, it's essential that we recognize and challenge these biases before they shape our decisions. Without realizing it, we may misinterpret student behavior, leading to punitive responses for what is simply a different way of engaging with the material.

The Teacher LENS Framework

In Chapter 2, we introduced the Teacher VIBE mindset. Building on that, the Teacher LENS is a practical tool for fostering a culturally responsive classroom where both individualistic and collectivistic values thrive.

The Teacher LENS encourages educators to do the following:

- Observe student behavior through a culturally sensitive lens.
- Identify potential mismatches between their expectations and students' cultural norms.
- Adapt strategies to honor diverse ways of processing and engaging with information to create a more inclusive classroom.

The framework consists of four components:

- L: Look for biases.
- E: Examine verbal and nonverbal communication.
- N: Notice group dynamics.
- S: Shift perspectives and interpret behavior.

Let's take a closer look at each component.

Look for Biases

Focus: Before observing your students, take a moment to reflect on your own potential biases. We all have assumptions about what a "well-behaved" or "engaged" student should look like. These biases often stem from our cultural backgrounds and teaching experiences.

Cultural implication: Your biases can cloud your understanding of student behavior, leading to misunderstandings or misjudgments. For example, what you perceive as disruptive might be a culturally appropriate way of engaging or communicating. Recognizing your own biases can help you create a more empathetic and inclusive classroom environment.

Questions:

- What cultural norms do I prioritize in my classroom (e.g., independence, silence, competition)?
- How might these norms influence my perception of student behavior?
- Am I open to behaviors that challenge my cultural expectations?

Examine Verbal and Nonverbal Communication

Focus: Pay close attention to how students interact verbally and nonverbally. Verbal processing—talking through ideas and problems—is a key learning strategy in many cultures. Nonverbal cues, such as eye contact, gestures, or body language, may also carry significant cultural meaning.

Cultural implication: Students from different backgrounds may express engagement, respect, or frustration in ways that differ from your expectations. For example, in some cultures, avoiding eye contact might be a sign of respect rather than disengagement.

Questions:

- Are students verbally processing their thoughts individually or in groups?
- How do students use body language or gestures to communicate?
- How do students engage nonverbally (e.g., eye contact, posture, proximity)?

Notice Group Dynamics

Focus: Observe how students interact during group tasks. In collectivist cultures, collaboration, mutual support, and group success are highly valued. Students may naturally share ideas and help one another solve problems.

Cultural implication: Traditional classroom management often emphasizes individual work and quiet compliance, which can stifle students from collectivist cultures. Observing group dynamics can help you create opportunities for collective learning that align with their strengths.

Questions:

- Are students helping and supporting one another in group tasks?
- How are ideas shared and discussed during collaborative activities?
- Do students appear more engaged in group activities compared to individual activities?

Shift Perspectives and Interpret Behavior

Focus: When you encounter behavior that seems off task or disruptive, pause and consider whether it might be culturally influenced. Reframing your interpretation through a cultural lens can lead to greater understanding and prevent unnecessary conflict.

Cultural implication: Shifting your perspective helps reduce the risk of misjudging students who are simply responding to their cultural norms. This approach fosters a more inclusive environment where all students feel respected and understood.

Questions:

- Is the behavior I'm observing truly disruptive, or is it culturally appropriate (e.g., talking during group problem solving)?

- How can I adjust my teaching strategies to better accommodate these cultural differences?
- What changes can I make to support a more inclusive learning environment?

Observing with Purpose

Using the Teacher LENS framework allows you to see beyond the surface of student behavior. By looking for biases, examining verbal and nonverbal communication, noticing group dynamics, and shifting your perspective, you can gain a deeper understanding of your students' cultural needs. Incorporating this approach into your daily practice will not only help you better interpret behaviors but also strengthen your classroom community by creating a space where all students feel valued and understood. In the next section, we'll explore practical examples and activities to help you put the Teacher LENS into action and ensure every student thrives in your classroom.

Using the LENS to Reduce Misinterpretations of Behavior

As we transition from traditional classroom management to cultivating our Teacher VIBE and using the Teacher LENS for observation, it's critical to remember that behavior is not just a response to rules; it's an expression of students' cultural norms, values, and ways of processing the world. When students and teachers come from different cultural backgrounds, behaviors that are normal and respectful in one context may be misinterpreted as disruptive or inappropriate in another.

Take, for example, Jason and Ms. Thompson from Chapter 1. Their disconnect led to tension, misunderstandings, and punitive measures against Jason because his teacher viewed his behavior through her own cultural lens. This affected Jason's academic and social development, highlighting the need for teachers to interpret behavior through a culturally responsive framework.

Using the LENS framework, we can reduce the number of these misinterpretations. The framework encourages teachers to move beyond surface-level observations and adopt a more inclusive perspective, fostering a classroom environment where all students feel accepted, supported, and included.

Individualistic and Collectivist Cultural Norms in Behavior

Understanding the cultural background that influences behavior can illuminate why certain actions occur in the classroom. It's worth revisiting the main characteristics of individualistic and collectivist cultures.

In the United States and many Western educational systems, individualism is emphasized. Students are encouraged to work independently, assert their opinions, and compete with peers for recognition and achievement. Classroom rules in these settings often prioritize quiet, independent work and self-reliance. Silence and personal space are typically associated with respect and focus.

In collectivist or communal cultures, often found in parts of Africa, Asia, Latin America, and the Caribbean, the focus is on group success, collaboration, and verbal communication as tools for collective problem solving. Students are encouraged to work together, share ideas, and support one another. Silence might be seen as disengagement or isolation, whereas talking and group interactions signify involvement and engagement.

Talking Out of Turn and Verbal Processing

In many communal cultures, verbal processing—talking through problems and sharing ideas aloud—is a natural and encouraged way to learn. Students might discuss assignments with peers, offer spontaneous answers, or share their thoughts aloud during work time. For them, conversation is a tool for understanding and engaging deeply with the material.

In individualistic classrooms, where quiet and independent work is often the standard, this behavior might be perceived as disruptive. Teachers may view it as a lack of discipline, focus, or respect for classroom rules.

Here's how the Teacher LENS can help interpret verbal processing inclusively:

- **Look for biases.** Ask yourself the following questions:
  — Do I expect quiet students to be more respectful or engaged?
  — Am I equating silence with focus and verbal engagement with disruption?

Recognizing and addressing these biases will help you better understand the value of verbal processing as a legitimate learning tool.

- **Examine verbal and nonverbal communication.** Pay attention to how students use language and body language. Students engaging in verbal processing may do the following:
  — Ask questions aloud or engage peers in dialogue.
  — Use animated gestures or facial expressions while thinking.

These are signs of active engagement, not disrespect.

- **Notice group dynamics.** Observe whether students' verbal processing contributes to collective learning. Are they engaged in any of the following behaviors?
    - Sharing ideas with peers?
    - Helping others solve problems?
    - Encouraging their classmates to participate?

These behaviors reflect communal learning values and often foster group success.

- **Shift perspectives and interpret behavior.** When faced with "talking out of turn," pause before reacting. Ask yourself the following questions:
    - Is this behavior truly disruptive, or is it a culturally influenced way of engaging?
    - How can I adjust my classroom norms to honor verbal processing while maintaining a positive learning environment?

Reframing your interpretation helps validate cultural expressions of engagement while creating space for students to thrive.

Helping Peers as a Collaborative Behavior

Another behavior often misinterpreted in individualistic classrooms is helping peers during tasks. In communal cultures, helping one another is a core value. It shows care for the community and a commitment to group success. Students may share answers, offer tips, or actively support struggling classmates.

In traditional classrooms, this behavior can be viewed as "cheating" or an inability to work independently. Teachers may see it as a failure to follow instructions, which can lead to disciplinary measures or lower grades.

Here's how the Teacher LENS can help interpret helping peers in a culturally inclusive way:

- **Look for biases.** Reflect on whether your classroom rules penalize collaboration unnecessarily. Are students being punished for behaviors that align with their cultural values?
- **Examine verbal and nonverbal communication.** Notice how students engage when helping peers. Are they reinforcing understanding or simply copying answers?
- **Notice group dynamics.** Watch how "helping behaviors" strengthen group cohesion and learning outcomes.
- **Shift perspectives and interpret behavior.** Instead of labeling these actions as "cheating," recognize them as signs of collectivist values and adapt classroom norms to allow peer-to-peer support.

Building Bridges Through Observation

The LENS framework offers a path to understanding and honoring the diverse behaviors in your classroom. By looking beyond surface-level interpretations, you can reduce misunderstandings, create a more inclusive environment, and validate the cultural norms your students bring to the classroom.

These efforts align with the Teacher VIBE mindset of Valuing Inclusion and Belonging for Everyone. By integrating this approach into your teaching, you ensure that all students—regardless of their cultural backgrounds—feel supported, respected, and empowered to learn.

In the next section, we'll explore practical strategies for using the LENS framework to interpret common classroom scenarios and provide actionable steps for creating culturally responsive learning environments.

A Sidenote for Individualist Teachers

I know the idea of allowing students to "talk out of turn" may put some teachers out of their comfort zone. I once observed a history lesson on colonization taught by a non-Native teacher to a group of Native American students on a reservation. While the teacher was speaking to the class, one student interrupted and asked, "How does it make you feel knowing that your people put us on this reservation?"

The teacher appeared caught off guard and visibly uncomfortable, and he pretended not to hear the question. He responded, "What did you say?" Another student immediately chimed in, "You heard him. How does it make you feel knowing your people put us on this reservation?"

Clearly unsure of how to respond and feeling uncomfortable with the question, the teacher shut down the conversation by saying, "Aw, we're not going to talk about that. I know what you're trying to do." From that point on, the lesson unraveled. The students pulled out their phones, passed notes, and completely disengaged from the rest of the class.

The next day, during our debrief, I asked the teacher why he had shut down the conversation. He explained that he felt uncomfortable with their questions, interpreting them as a challenge to his authority.

I agreed that he was being challenged but reminded him of a few key points. First, the students' questions were directly on topic; they were engaging in a conversation about colonization. Second, because he was a non-Native teacher on the reservation, the students wanted to know his intentions in working within their community and how he viewed them. A simple response like "You know what, I'm sorry that this happened to your people, and I recognize that historically, these situations have deeply affected your community" would have validated their feelings and shown respect. A response such as this could have helped build trust and rapport. Finally, I reminded him that he was a guest within their community, which values a collectivist approach. Although they were challenging him, they were also engaging in the lesson. He immediately interpreted their directness as disrespectful, but in their culture, challenging authority can be a form of engagement, not defiance.

This example provides the following takeaways for teachers working in collectivist environments:

- **Understand that engagement may look different.** In collectivist cultures, students may express their engagement in ways that can be unfamiliar to those from an individualistic background. Rather than seeing challenges or direct questions as defiance, recognize them as opportunities for deeper dialogue and learning. A response like "thank you for your question; let's unpack that" invites students to engage in a discussion and confirms their value within the classroom community. In these environments, collective discussions are often how students process and engage with complex topics.
- **Be ready to address cultural and historical contexts.** In any culturally diverse setting, students may ask questions about historical injustices or the impact of your background on the subject matter. Instead of shutting down such discussions, use them as teachable moments. Acknowledging students' perspectives and concerns demonstrates respect and builds trust.

(continued)

- **Foster open dialogue.** Create an environment where students feel comfortable expressing themselves, even when their questions or comments challenge your perspective. In collectivist settings, discussions are often communal and inclusive, and by fostering open dialogue, you can facilitate more meaningful engagement.
- **Recognize the role of relationships.** In collectivist cultures, building strong, respectful relationships is essential. A teacher who takes the time to understand and connect with their students' cultural background can foster a more collaborative and productive learning environment. When students feel respected, they are more likely to stay engaged and invest in the learning process.

Using the LENS Framework: Sample Scenarios

Understanding the elements and general benefits of the LENS framework provides the foundation for further exploration of this tool. Now let's look at some examples of how it might operate in specific situations.

Verbal Processing in Group Activities

In Ms. Carter's 3rd grade math class, Amir, a student from a collectivist culture, begins discussing strategies with his tablemate during a group activity. The instructions require students to write their answers individually before sharing with the group. Amir leans over to José and asks, "Is this the right way?" while pointing to his work. Ms. Carter, expecting each student to complete their work quietly and independently, interprets Amir's behavior as rushing ahead or not following instructions.

Here's how the LENS might be applied in this scenario:

- **Examine verbal and nonverbal communication.** Ms. Carter can observe Amir's behavior more closely to understand its intent. Is he confused or not paying attention, or is he actively engaging in a way that reflects how he processes information best?
- **Interpretation:** Amir's question to José isn't about bypassing the process but reflects his cultural tendency to learn collaboratively by confirming his understanding with peers. By recognizing this, Ms. Carter can adjust her approach, validating Amir's cultural preference while gently guiding him toward the activity's expectations. (Peer assessments, a strategy discussed in Chapter 5, could help align these cultural preferences with classroom objectives.)

Helping Peers and Collective Problem Solving

Working on an 8th grade writing assignment, Janelle, a student from a communal, or collectivist, culture, walks over to check on a classmate's progress, offering suggestions and encouragement. In an individualistic setting, this behavior might be perceived as inappropriate or as a form of academic dishonesty because it disrupts the focus on individual work.

Here's how the LENS might be applied in this scenario:

- **Notice group dynamics.** Janelle's actions reflect her cultural value of mutual support and the belief that group success is paramount. Observing her interactions might reveal that her intention is to ensure no one feels left behind rather than to undermine the task.

- **Interpretation:** Instead of reprimanding Janelle, the teacher could channel this behavior positively by allowing structured peer support sessions or creating collaborative checkpoints. This approach would honor Janelle's cultural values while maintaining academic integrity.

Group Discussions and Verbal Engagement

During a group discussion in a history class, students from a communal culture interject during a peer's presentation, asking questions and offering insights spontaneously. From Mr. Garcia's perspective, this behavior seems interruptive and disrespectful to classroom norms. However, for these students, verbal back-and-forth exchanges reflect intellectual collaboration and are seen as respectful contributions.

Here's how the LENS might be applied in this scenario:

- **Shift perspectives and interpret behavior.** Instead of viewing these interjections as disruptions, Mr. Garcia can reframe them as active engagement. He could ask himself the following questions:
    - Are students demonstrating curiosity and collaboration through their questions and comments?
    - How can this verbal engagement be structured to encourage shared understanding without disrupting classroom order?
- **Interpretation:** Mr. Garcia could establish norms that balance open discussions with turn-taking, creating a space where both individualistic and collectivist students feel heard and valued.

Key Takeaways

By applying the LENS framework to these scenarios, teachers can do the following:

- Recognize the cultural underpinnings of student behavior.
- Avoid punitive measures for actions rooted in cultural norms.
- Foster a classroom environment where all students feel accepted, supported, and included.

These examples highlight the importance of cultural responsiveness: What may seem like noncompliance or disruption is often a reflection of diverse ways of learning and engaging. Teachers equipped with the LENS framework can move toward more inclusive practices that empower every student.

Understanding Communication Styles Through the LENS Framework

Classroom behaviors that are misunderstood often arise from differences in cultural communication styles, including factors such as eye contact, tone of voice, and the broader factor of indirect versus direct communication, particularly in terms of giving feedback and asking questions. Let's explore common cultural misunderstandings and how the LENS framework can help educators interpret these behaviors more accurately. (Figure 3.1 summarizes the main points.)

Direct Eye Contact Versus Avoidance

In many Western cultures, direct eye contact symbolizes attentiveness, respect, and honesty (Haensel et al., 2021). This expectation is often taught at an early age, as parents encourage their children to "look people in the eyes" during conversations or handshakes. However, in many communal cultures, avoiding eye contact can signify deference, humility, or respect, especially when interacting with elders or authority figures.

Consider this scenario: Mr. Kelley notices that Jessie avoids eye contact during a one-on-one conversation. He interprets

FIGURE 3.1
Applying the LENS Framework to Cultural Misunderstandings

Misunderstanding	Example	LENS Application
Eye contact versus avoidance	Avoiding eye contact is seen as disengagement but actually shows respect.	• Look for biases: Question assumptions about eye contact. • Examine communication: Observe body language for signs of engagement. • Shift perspectives: View avoidance as a sign of cultural respect.
Tone of voice	Loud speaking is seen as aggression but shows enthusiasm in some cultures.	• Look for biases: Reflect on preferences for a quieter tone. • Examine communication: Recognize passion, not disruption. • Shift perspectives: Reframe loudness as a sign of engagement.
Indirect versus direct communication	Hesitation is seen as lack of initiative but reflects respect.	• Look for biases: Question expectations of directness. • Examine communication: Notice indirect cues of confusion. • Shift perspectives: Understand hesitation as a sign of cultural respect.

this as Jessie being disengaged, disinterested, or even guilty of wrongdoing. However, Jessie's behavior may actually reflect her cultural norm of showing respect by avoiding direct eye contact with authority figures.

Here's how the LENS might be applied in this scenario:

- **Look for biases.** Mr. Kelley should reflect on whether his assumption—that direct eye contact universally conveys respect—might be leading him to misinterpret Jessie's behavior.
- **Examine verbal and nonverbal communication.** Jessie's body language, tone, and attentiveness during the conversation might indicate engagement, even if she avoids direct eye contact.

- **Shift perspectives and interpret behavior.** Instead of assuming disengagement, Mr. Kelley should recognize Jessie's behavior as culturally appropriate and adjust his expectations during such interactions.

Tone of Voice

In some cultures, speaking loudly, passionately, and with expressive gestures is the norm, particularly when debating or discussing ideas (Zhang & Pell, 2022). This speaking style contrasts with the style common in cultures in which a softer, more subdued tone reflects politeness and respect. Teachers accustomed to quieter communication may misinterpret louder voices as aggressive or confrontational.

Consider this scenario: During a class discussion, Wilson and Chelsea, who come from cultures that value impassioned dialogue, raise their voices while debating a topic. Mr. Osborne perceives their volume as disruptive or confrontational, even though Wilson and Chelsea are simply engaging in their culturally familiar way of expressing enthusiasm.

Here's how the LENS might be applied in this scenario:

- **Look for biases.** Mr. Osborne should reflect on his preference for quieter discussions and consider whether it causes him to misinterpret louder tones as disruptive.
- **Examine verbal and nonverbal communication.** By observing Wilson and Chelsea's body language, tone, and overall demeanor, Mr. Osborne can identify whether their raised voices indicate excitement rather than conflict.
- **Notice group dynamics.** Paying attention to whether other students from similar backgrounds engage in similar ways can help Mr. Osborne understand that this communication style is culturally appropriate.

- **Shift perspectives and interpret behavior.** Mr. Osborne can embrace different communication styles by encouraging all students to share ideas in ways that feel natural to them, while also setting norms that ensure discussions remain respectful.

Indirect Versus Direct Communication Styles

Cultures differ in how they approach communication, particularly in giving feedback or asking questions. In some cultures, indirect communication—hinting at a need rather than explicitly stating it—is common, especially when there is uncertainty or a hierarchical dynamic at play. In contrast, U.S. classrooms often emphasize direct communication, where students are encouraged to speak up clearly.

Consider the following scenario: Mya hesitates to directly ask Ms. Coleman for clarification about an assignment. Instead, she hints at her confusion through body language or indirect comments. Ms. Coleman interprets Mya's hesitation as a lack of interest or initiative, rather than understanding that Mya's cultural norms may discourage direct questioning.

Here's how the LENS might be applied in this scenario:

- **Look for biases.** Ms. Coleman should examine whether her preference for direct communication is causing her to misinterpret Mya's behavior as disengaged.
- **Examine verbal and nonverbal communication.** Observing Mya's hesitation, softer tone, or reliance on nonverbal cues like facial expressions can provide insight into her uncertainty.
- **Shift perspectives and interpret behavior.** Understanding that Mya's indirect communication may stem from cultural norms, Ms. Coleman can adjust her approach by

creating open-ended opportunities for students to express confusion, such as encouraging anonymous questions or offering one-on-one check-ins.

By using the LENS framework, teachers can better understand the cultural underpinnings of their students' communication styles. This approach helps reduce misunderstandings, builds trust, and fosters a more inclusive learning environment where all students feel accepted, supported, and empowered to express themselves.

Strategies for Using the Teacher LENS

As noted throughout this chapter, behavior that we perceive as disruptive or inappropriate often has deeper cultural context and intention behind it. Unfortunately, students from communal backgrounds are often reprimanded for "breaking the rules" when, in fact, they are engaging in ways that are natural and familiar to them. Strengthening your Teacher VIBE means using your Teacher LENS to view behavior through a cultural lens, helping you respond with understanding rather than assumption. Here are five key strategies for using the Teacher LENS:

1. **Take a moment to pause and reflect before reacting (Look for biases).** When a student's behavior appears off-task or disruptive, resist the urge to react immediately. Ask yourself whether the student might be responding to cultural norms different from your expectations. Recognizing your own biases allows you to maintain positive relationships while preventing unnecessary conflict.
2. **Engage in active listening (Examine verbal and nonverbal communication).** Listen not only to what students say but also to *how* they say it. Tone, context, and intent

matter. Are students verbally processing ideas as part of how they engage with and make sense of the content? Are they expressing excitement with a louder tone or gestures that might seem out of place in a traditional classroom? Recognizing these cues helps you better understand their engagement.

3. **Learn about your students' cultural backgrounds (Notice group dynamics).** Understanding students' cultural contexts can help you interpret their behaviors accurately. Take time to learn about their traditions, values, and community practices. Engage families and community members in conversations to gain deeper insights. Asking questions like "What's a meaningful tradition in your family?" creates opportunities for meaningful dialogue and prevents assumptions.

4. **Use culturally responsive strategies (Shift perspectives and interpret behavior).** Adapt your teaching practices to incorporate strategies that align with students' cultural norms. Include more group discussions for collectivist learners or allow verbal processing for students who learn through dialogue. Create flexible environments that encourage students to engage in ways that feel natural and valued.

5. **Offer flexible classroom expectations.** Evaluate whether your classroom rules align with your students' cultural values. For example, instead of enforcing complete silence during independent work, allow quiet discussions or verbal problem solving. Incorporate collaborative activities like project-based learning to honor collective success. This flexibility can create an environment where students feel comfortable and engaged without compromising their cultural identity.

Summing Up and Looking Ahead

In this chapter, we explored the importance of interpreting student behavior through a cultural lens. The Teacher LENS framework equips educators with the tools to move beyond assumptions and build a classroom where all students feel accepted, supported, and included.

Cultural contexts influence behavior, and what may initially seem like disengagement or disruption could simply be students expressing themselves naturally. By applying the LENS, educators can avoid misunderstandings, strengthen student–teacher relationships, and cultivate an inclusive environment that values diverse cultural expressions.

Ultimately, observing through a culturally responsive lens requires curiosity, adaptability, and a commitment to honoring students' unique perspectives. The goal isn't to enforce compliance but to embrace the richness of cultural diversity in ways that empower every student to thrive authentically.

In the next chapter, we'll explore innovative methods to engage collectivist students, including project-based learning, storytelling, gamification, and other strategies that foster collaboration and inclusivity. You'll gain practical tools to adapt these approaches to your unique classroom needs, ensuring that all students feel engaged and valued in the learning process.

4

Incorporating Teaching Techniques for Today's Classroom

I might be dating myself, but let me take you back in time for a moment. I'm an '80s baby, and like many from my generation, I was hooked on Nintendo. My favorite of all time? *The Legend of Zelda*. If you had a Nintendo back then, you might remember how *Zelda* revolutionized the gaming world. Yes, we still had to blow on the cartridges to get the games to play, but there was a key gaming feature that took the Nintendo to the next level.

Before *Zelda* came out, we had games like *Super Mario Bros.*, which required that you play straight through. When you turned on the game, you were in for the long haul; if you wanted to beat King Koopa, you needed to dedicate hours. And if you lost, well, you had to start over again. There was no saving your progress, outside of hitting "pause"; there was no coming back later to pick up where you left off.

Then came *Zelda*, and everything changed. It wasn't just another game; it was a game-changer—literally. It came in a shiny gold cartridge, which was something we'd never seen before, as the typical game cartridge was gray. I suspect Nintendo knew they had a masterpiece on their hands and wanted to set it apart from the other games. But what blew our minds was the ability to save your game. You could create a profile, return to the game later, and continue your adventure right where you left off. It was innovative and forward-thinking, and it redefined what gaming could be. That simple shift—from playing in one session to saving progress—revolutionized our engagement with games.

Now, you might be wondering why I'm bringing this up. The reason is that just like *Zelda* pushed video games into a new era, it's time for teaching to transform. Just as *Zelda* introduced a more immersive, long-term approach to gaming, we as educators must shift from a one-size-fits-all, individualistic-focused approach to a more innovative, collectivist one that recognizes the power of community and shared experiences in the classroom.

In the same way that *Zelda* allowed players to save their progress and continue their journey over time, a collectivist classroom allows students to build on each other's knowledge and experiences, creating an environment where learning is a shared, ongoing process. Structuring lessons and activities in which students collaborate, can pick up where they left off, and use their character avatar strengths, supports a sense of belonging and adds to your Teacher VIBE. We must embrace opportunities for incorporating newer teaching practices as we facilitate a student-centered classroom. Just as *Zelda* transformed gaming, we can transform our classrooms by moving from a focus on individual achievement to fostering a sense of community and collective growth.

This chapter will introduce you to three powerful teaching practices that will help you elevate your Teacher VIBE and make this shift. We'll explore how project-based learning (PBL), storytelling (or "storifying"), and gamification can create a more dynamic, collaborative classroom environment. Each of these strategies encourages students to learn together, share their strengths, and build on collective insights—taking your teaching to the next level and ensuring that every student feels accepted, supported, and included on the journey.

Connecting Cultures and Classrooms Through Project-Based Learning

Project-based learning is a teaching practice that transcends traditional group assignments, creating meaningful and deeper learning experiences by connecting classroom content with students' lives outside school. Understanding how PBL intersects with equity and cultural contexts is essential for strengthening your Teacher VIBE. In this section, I'll share how PBL fosters belonging on a culturally responsive level and how this approach benefits both individualistic and collectivist cultures.

Understanding PBL

At its core, PBL focuses on learning through inquiry, problem solving, and real-world application (Eakins, 2024b). Unlike traditional teaching methods, which assign projects as an add-on at the end of a unit, PBL starts with an essential question or challenge that students work toward solving throughout the learning process. The project is not just an activity; it becomes the central method through which students engage with the content and develop skills (Almulla, 2020).

One of the myths about PBL is that it is synonymous with group work, which might cause concern for individualistic students. However, PBL involves more than just creating engaging projects; it's about designing learning experiences that connect with students' realities and allow flexibility in how they engage. Teachers can implement PBL with individual students or groups, ensuring that different ways of processing and engaging with information are supported.

For PBL to succeed, teachers must design projects with a deep understanding of their students (Eakins, 2024b), which requires intentionally learning about students' communities, cultures, languages, and individual strengths. It's essential to avoid relying on stereotypes when determining who your students are. Taking time to build relationships with your students will help you identify the best PBL opportunities for your classroom while saving time in the long run.

Why You Should Consider PBL

One of PBL's greatest strengths is its ability to foster a sense of belonging. But what does belonging look like in a PBL classroom? It begins with recognizing and deeply understanding the diverse needs, strengths, and identities of your students. Understanding goes beyond simply knowing students' names, reading levels, or test scores. It requires seeing your students holistically—what excites them, what they care about, and how they interact with the world.

You can gather this information in various ways, such as interest surveys, skills inventories, or applying the LENS observational framework introduced in Chapter 3 (Look for biases, Examine verbal and nonverbal communication, Notice group dynamics, and Shift perspectives and interpret behavior). This approach ensures you understand your students beyond the data—identifying their values, lived experiences, and preferred ways of learning.

When teachers engage in this level of understanding, they can design projects that not only align with content standards but also resonate with students' realities and interests. This effort fosters meaningful engagement, making students feel seen and valued in the learning process.

First-Day Activity: Classroom Bingo

To set the stage for effective PBL, it's important to start building connections from day one. Classroom Bingo is a fun and interactive activity that helps students learn about each other's strengths, interests, and identities while fostering a sense of belonging. Here's how it works:

1. **Create a bingo card.** Design a card with prompts such as these:
   — Find someone who loves solving puzzles.
   — Find someone who prefers working alone.
   — Find someone who enjoys storytelling.
   — Find someone who speaks more than one language.
   — Find someone who wants to be a team leader.
2. **Play the game.** Give students time to mingle, asking their classmates questions to complete their bingo card. Encourage them to talk with as many people as possible, creating a lively and inclusive atmosphere.
3. **Reflect and discuss.** Once the activity is complete, lead a group discussion. Ask students to share what they learned about their classmates. What similarities did they notice? What new insights did they gain about their peers?

Classroom Bingo can lead to various benefits, including the following:

- It helps students discover commonalities, setting the foundation for collaboration.
- It provides a way for teachers to gain valuable insights into students' preferences, strengths, and cultural identities.
- It fosters an inclusive classroom community from the very beginning of the school year.
- The information gathered can serve as a "cheat sheet" for assigning roles in future PBL activities, ensuring that students can contribute in ways that align with their strengths.

By incorporating activities like Classroom Bingo (see Figure 4.1 for a sample card), you set the foundation for a classroom culture where PBL can thrive and every student has a voice. It's not just about completing a project; it's about creating a community of learners who support and celebrate each other's unique contributions.

FIGURE 4.1
Sample Classroom Bingo Card

B	I	N	G	O
Likes to be a group leader	Prefers working in pairs	Enjoys creative problem solving	Is interested in technology	Loves art or design
Speaks two or more languages	Has done community service	Plays a musical instrument	Likes writing down their ideas	Loves organizing things
Feels confident presenting	Enjoys researching things	Plays a team sport	Likes hands-on projects	Cares about community issues
Has been a team captain before	Is curious about how things work	Prefers working alone	Is passionate about equal treatment	Loves learning about different cultures

First-Day Activity: "Getting to Know You" Student Questionnaire

A "getting to know you" survey is a helpful tool you can use to learn things about your students beyond their academic skills. Like Classroom Bingo, it's another way to learn your students' strengths, interests, and cultural preferences, giving you the opportunity to personalize projects that will interest them. Learning your students' preferred methods of communication, collaboration, and problem-solving strategies puts you on the right path toward creating a sense of belonging. Use these data; don't sit on them. Again, the frontloading will save you so much time in the end, and you'll have what you need for culturally responsive projects that keep your students engaged.

Here are some suggestions for items to include in a questionnaire to distribute on the first day of school:

- What subjects or activities do you enjoy the most at school? Why?
- When you work on a project, what part excites you the most (e.g., planning, organizing, building, presenting, researching)?
- How do you feel most comfortable sharing your ideas (e.g., in writing, speaking to a group, making videos, creating artwork)?
- Do you prefer working in small groups, large groups, pairs, or individually? Why?
- What is something you care deeply about or are passionate about (in or outside school)?
- When you need to solve a problem, what strategies do you use?

- What are some things you would like your teacher to know about you? (This could be about how you learn best, your strengths, your hobbies, or anything else.)
- Have you ever worked on a project that made a difference in your school or community? What was it?
- How do you like to receive feedback on your work (e.g., written notes, one-on-one conversations, peer feedback)?
- Is there anything else you'd like to share about how you like to learn or work with others?

Individualistic and Collectivist Cultures in PBL

Believe it or not, one key quality of PBL is its adaptability to both individualistic and collectivist cultures. For students from individualistic backgrounds, PBL offers opportunities to work on independent projects that allow them to showcase their unique perspectives, creativity, or skills (Eakins, 2024b). These opportunities could include presenting ideas in various formats, such as oral presentations, written reflections, or multimedia projects. By providing diverse avenues for students to demonstrate their understanding, you ensure that all voices are heard and valued in ways that resonate with their personal learning preferences.

For collectivist students, PBL naturally aligns with their strengths in group work and collaboration. In these settings, students come together in pairs, small groups, or as a whole class to solve complex problems, share resources, and support one another. They can contribute their unique strengths to achieve a shared goal (Eakins, 2024b). This cooperative effort mirrors the communal values of collectivist cultures, fostering a sense of belonging and shared accomplishment.

Because of its flexibility, PBL supports both individual and collaborative approaches to processing information. Whether students prefer working independently or thrive in collaborative settings, PBL can be tailored to meet their needs, ensuring that all students have meaningful opportunities to contribute and learn within their cultural context.

Building Collaborative and Individual Accountability

A common question that arises with PBL is "How do I ensure that all students contribute equally?" Managing group dynamics is crucial for the success of collaborative projects, and it starts with establishing clear protocols for collaboration. This process can be integrated into the creation of your classroom community agreement (see Chapter 2). If PBL is a consistent part of your instructional practice—and it should be if you aim to strengthen your Teacher VIBE—it's essential to invest time in setting clear team expectations and procedures. This effort not only strengthens your classroom community but also prepares students for future scenarios where effective teamwork and communication are critical.

Whereas group protocols are essential, balancing collaborative projects with opportunities for individual accountability is equally important. Even in group settings, students should have the chance to demonstrate their personal contributions and learning. Here are some suggestions for how to create such opportunities:

- Assign individual roles within the larger group project.
- Include individual reflections or assessments on what each student learned or contributed.

These measures ensure that every student is recognized for their efforts and that the learning experience remains equitable.

An Opportunity to Be Culturally Responsive

One of PBL's most significant benefits is its potential to foster cultural responsiveness. By building relationships with your students and understanding their unique backgrounds, you can design projects that are relevant and relatable to their lived experiences. PBL provides a platform to amplify student voices and integrate their cultural contexts into the learning process.

Here are ways to make PBL culturally responsive:

- Pose questions such as "Whose voices are missing from this narrative?" or "What perspectives have been overlooked?"
- Design projects that explore Indigenous histories, amplify local community strengths, or challenge students to examine issues like power and privilege within their communities.

Culturally grounded projects that incorporate these suggestions not only teach academic content but also empower students to become critical thinkers and active participants in shaping a more socially just world.

The Power of Thoughtful Planning

Thoughtful planning is the foundation of successful PBL. Without intentional design, PBL risks becoming just another group assignment rather than the transformative learning experience it has the potential to be. Planning starts with understanding your students—their cultural contexts, individual needs, and collective dynamics—and aligning these insights with your learning objectives. Here are suggestions for planning and creating meaningful PBL experiences:

- Identify your students' strengths and interests early in the school year through surveys (e.g., following the suggestions

presented earlier in this chapter), conversations, or the LENS observational framework introduced in Chapter 3.
- Develop projects that connect classroom content to real-world challenges, ensuring relevance and engagement.
- Scaffold learning activities to support both individual and group contributions.

Well-planned PBL fosters belonging and connection while helping students see the relevance of their learning in their lives and communities. By weaving these experiences throughout your teaching, rather than treating PBL as a "one and done" activity, you can make it an integral part of your practice, enriching your classroom environment and strengthening your Teacher VIBE.

At its heart, project-based learning is about creating a space where all students can thrive. Whether your students navigate individualistic or collectivist cultures, PBL can be a transformative tool for fostering deep engagement, collaboration, and self-discovery. By making PBL a consistent part of your teaching practice, you not only prepare your students to tackle complex challenges but also help them build the skills they need to engage meaningfully with the world around them. (See Figure 4.2 for some specific project ideas.)

Storytelling as a Road Map to the Future: Navigating Individualism and Collectivism

Incorporating storytelling into your curriculum does more than provide entertainment or engagement; it serves as a powerful road map to the future (Eakins, 2024a). Storytelling is a dynamic tool that bridges individualistic and collectivist cultural

FIGURE 4.2
PBL Ideas That Benefit Collectivists, with Modifications for Individualists

Activity	Overview	Benefit to Collectivist Students	Modifications for Individualistic Students
Community service projects	Students collaborate to design and implement a community project, such as organizing a charity event or recycling program.	They emphasize teamwork, shared goals, and contributing to the community.	Assign individual roles like project leader or media manager, and offer opportunities for personal reflection.
Cultural heritage exhibitions	Students create an exhibition showcasing cultural traditions, researching countries, artifacts, clothing, and music.	They encourage connection to cultural roots and promote respect for traditions.	Allow students to focus on their own heritage or lead specific exhibition areas, offering opportunities for solo presentation.
Collaborative science experiments	Groups design and conduct experiments, analyze results, and present findings on topics like plant growth or water purification.	They reinforce collective responsibility and ensure all students contribute to group success.	Assign specific roles like data analyst or experiment designer, and allow for individual reports and reflections.
School or classroom garden project	Students work together to plan, design, and maintain a garden, involving tasks such as planting, watering, and creating signage.	It fosters collaboration and shared responsibility for long-term efforts.	Offer leadership roles like project manager or plant expert, and include reflective journals for personal contributions.
Documentary film project	Students collaborate to produce a documentary on a social issue or historical event, handling tasks like research, filming, and editing.	It promotes teamwork and cooperation through roles like videographer, editor, and scriptwriter.	Assign individual responsibilities like directing or editing, and allow for independent interviews or personal commentaries.

(continued)

FIGURE 4.2
PBL Ideas That Benefit Collectivists, with Modifications for Individualists (*Continued*)

Activity	Overview	Benefit to Collectivist Students	Modifications for Individualistic Students
Entrepreneurial projects	Students form groups to design a business plan or simulate starting a company, including researching markets and creating a business model.	They encourage shared decision making and learning from one another to achieve collective success.	Assign leadership roles like CEO or CFO, and include opportunities for individual pitches or reflective evaluation of personal learning.
Historical reenactment or debate	Students reenact historical events or debate historical/contemporary issues, engaging in research, costume design, and role-playing.	It reinforces group work and cooperation in portraying historical events or constructing arguments for debate.	Provide opportunities for individual leadership roles in debates or reenactments, and recognize strong research or speaking skills.
Environmental action plan	Students develop a plan to address a local environmental issue, such as reducing plastic waste or promoting recycling.	It encourages a shared commitment to solving community problems and emphasizes ongoing collaboration.	Assign individual leadership roles in research or outreach, and allow for personal reflection on contributions and achievements.
Global pen pal or cultural exchange project	Students are paired with pen pals from another country, collaborating on projects like cultural research, writing letters, and hosting virtual meetings.	It promotes intercultural understanding and collaboration with students from different backgrounds.	Allow students to lead specific discussions or conduct independent research, and encourage reflective journaling or solo projects.

norms, allowing students to express themselves while honoring their unique backgrounds and cultural values. By integrating cultural storytelling into teaching and learning, you open a window into your students' experiences, enabling deeper connections and providing valuable insights into how they interact with the world.

Traditional curriculum and instruction often include a heavy focus on written content, which tends to favor individualistic approaches to learning and processing information. As you reflect on your current instructional and assessment practices, consider how you can balance them to embrace oral storytelling and collective narratives, creating more opportunities for your collectivist students to thrive. By doing so, you create an inclusive learning environment aligned with the Teacher VIBE.

Storytelling for Individualistic and Collectivist Students

For your students from individualistic cultures, storytelling provides a platform to share their unique experiences, thoughts, and perspectives. This practice leverages self-reflection and personal growth, helping these students develop their individual voices both figuratively and literally. Storytelling allows them to do the following:

- Explore their identity through personal narratives
- Share singular achievements or milestones
- Assert their independence by crafting and owning their stories

These activities tap into the values of independence and personal achievement, ensuring that students feel seen and validated for their individuality.

For your students from collectivist cultures, storytelling often goes beyond self-expression; it is a way to honor the collective. These students may view their identities as deeply intertwined with their families, communities, and broader social networks. Their stories might focus on topics such as these:

- Family history and shared experiences
- Communal values and cultural traditions
- Collective achievements that highlight the importance of group harmony and interdependence

Many collectivist cultures hold oral storytelling as a revered tradition, a way to pass down lessons, values, and history from one generation to the next (see Figure 4.3 for specific examples of such cultures). By incorporating storytelling into your classroom, you validate these cultural practices and reinforce a sense of belonging for students who come from oral traditions.

Storytelling is a versatile teaching practice that supports your Teacher VIBE by balancing the needs of individualistic and collectivist learners. It allows all students to connect their personal and collective experiences to the curriculum, fostering a deeper sense of belonging and engagement. Whether students are sharing their own achievements or celebrating the traditions of their communities, storytelling creates a classroom environment where every voice is valued and every story matters.

As you develop your VIBE mindset, it's crucial to recognize these differences and use storytelling as a bridge between both perspectives. This will allow all students to explore their identities and experiences in ways that resonate with them culturally.

FIGURE 4.3
Examples of Cultures That Revere Oral Storytelling

Culture	Region	Significance of Oral Storytelling
Indigenous cultures	North America, Australia	Oral storytelling conveys history, values, cosmology, and laws across generations. It is central to the preservation of cultural identity (Ranco & Haverkamp, 2022).
West African cultures	West Africa (Mali, Senegal, Guinea)	Griots serve as storytellers, historians, and musicians, preserving cultural knowledge through the spoken word, including genealogies and important legends (Poku, 2022).
Celtic cultures	Ireland, Scotland, Wales	Bards and poets were revered figures who passed down myths, legends, folklore, and histories, maintaining cultural continuity in times before written records (Zamani, 2022).
Hawaiian (Polynesian) culture	Hawaii	Oral storytelling, combined with hula and chants, was a key way of sharing genealogies, histories, and ancestral wisdom (Reilly, 2023).
Māori culture	New Zealand	Whakapapa involves oral storytelling of genealogies, histories, and tribal lore, with elders playing a vital role in transmitting knowledge (Jackson et al., 2024).
Yoruba culture	Nigeria	Oral storytelling preserves history and cultural identity, with proverbs, folktales, and mythological accounts imparting moral lessons and historical knowledge (Atiku, 2021).
Inuit and Arctic Indigenous cultures	Arctic regions (Inuit)	Legends and myths about survival, nature, and the spirit world are passed down orally, often providing practical lessons for life in harsh environments (Eerkes-Medrano & Huntington, 2021).
Pacific Islander cultures	Pacific Islands (Samoa, Tonga, Fiji)	Oral traditions include storytelling, chants, and dances that pass down genealogies, cosmologies, and cultural knowledge related to nature and the ocean (Lilomaiava-Doktor, 2020).
Bedouin culture	Middle East, North Africa	Oral poetry and storytelling around heroism, love, and tribal history are key in preserving nomadic Bedouin culture and values (Berrebbah, 2020).
Ancient Greek culture	Greece	Before being written down, myths and heroic legends like *The Iliad* and *The Odyssey* were passed down through oral storytelling, maintaining Greek cultural continuity (Grethlein, 2023).

Breaking Barriers: Engaging Families from Different Cultural Perspectives

Storytelling provides a powerful avenue for breaking down barriers between school and home, particularly for collectivist families who value communal participation in their children's education (Qarooni, 2024). As a teacher, you may already encourage family engagement by inviting parents to share their backgrounds. However, it's essential to be mindful of cultural and language differences that might make some families hesitant to participate.

For example, I interviewed Nawal Qarooni on my *Leading Equity* podcast, where she shared a personal story about her mother, a native Farsi speaker, who hesitated when asked to be a guest "reader" in the classroom. The term *reader* felt formal and intimidating. However, when the role was reframed as *storyteller*, her mother felt more comfortable sharing family stories from Iran (Eakins, 2024a).

For collectivist families, terms like *reader* may imply a level of formality that feels disconnected from their cultural practices. By inviting families to participate as storytellers instead, you create a more inclusive and culturally responsive way to involve them in the classroom.

Storytelling offers an authentic, welcoming, and meaningful method for family engagement. When we embrace its communal aspect, we provide families with opportunities to connect with the classroom in ways that feel familiar and culturally significant.

Similarly, for families from individualistic cultures, storytelling can be a tool for personal reflection and self-expression. Students and families might focus more on telling stories that highlight personal achievements or unique perspectives, allowing their narratives to integrate seamlessly into the classroom's larger collective identity.

First-Day Activity: Five Things You Should Know About Me

The Five Things You Should Know About Me activity is an excellent way to help students introduce themselves at the start of the school year. Students bring in (or draw or write about) five objects that represent key aspects of their lives—such as personal achievements, family traditions, hobbies, or cultural heritage—and can serve as tools for storytelling. Individualistic students may focus on objects that represent their unique experiences, personal milestones, or hobbies. Collectivist students may choose objects that reflect family, community, or cultural traditions. The activity proceeds in the following four steps:

1. **Introduction.** Explain the purpose of the activity, highlighting how it helps the class learn about one another's identities, strengths, and interests.
2. **Preparation.** Give students time to think about their five objects. Provide examples to help them brainstorm.
3. **Sharing.** Students bring in and share their objects (or writings or drawings) with a partner, small group, or the entire class. Encourage them to explain why each object is meaningful.
4. **Reflection.** Facilitate a discussion about what students learned about one another, emphasizing connections and shared values.

This activity fosters inclusivity and encourages students to share their personal or communal experiences in ways that feel authentic and meaningful.

First-Day Activity: The Class Story Tree

The Class Story Tree is a whole-class project that helps create a sense of unity while celebrating each student's individuality. Each student contributes a branch to a collective tree, showcasing their personal stories, cultural heritage, and values. The activity emphasizes how individual and collective identities strengthen the classroom community. Here are the steps:

1. **Introduction (10 minutes)**: Explain the concept of the Class Story Tree. Emphasize that the trunk represents the classroom community and each branch symbolizes a unique student. Work with the class to develop a theme or mantra for the year, displayed prominently on the tree.
2. **Creating the tree (10 minutes)**: Draw or craft a large tree on poster paper, a bulletin board, or a wall. Leave the branches blank for students to add their contributions.
3. **Adding branches (20–30 minutes)**: Provide students with blank branch templates or cutouts. On their branch, students write or draw key aspects of their identity, including the following possibilities:
   — Cultural heritage or roots
   — Family traditions or values
   — Hobbies, interests, or achievements
   — Future goals or dreams

   Encourage students to decorate their branches with colors and symbols that reflect their personality.
4. **Sharing and connecting (20–30 minutes)**: Students present their branches, explaining the significance of their contributions before attaching them to the tree. Discuss how the branches come together to create a diverse yet unified classroom community.

5. **Reflection (10 minutes)**: Gather the class around the finished tree and facilitate a discussion around the following questions:
    — What did you learn about your classmates?
    — How does seeing all the branches together change your understanding of our classroom community?

Navigating Discomfort: The Challenges of Storytelling in a Diverse Classroom

Storytelling activities often reveal differences in students' experiences, particularly when diverse socioeconomic or cultural backgrounds come into play. For example, one student might share an elaborate story about a family vacation, whereas another might focus on the resilience and unity of their family through difficult times (Eakins, 2024a). Both stories hold value and meaning for the students sharing them, but these differences may evoke discomfort among peers unfamiliar with contrasting perspectives.

To navigate such moments, emphasize the value of the storytelling process over the final product. Create an environment where students feel encouraged to share their stories and where their narratives are respected as equal contributions to the classroom community. This approach ensures that both individual and collective narratives are honored without creating a sense of competition between them.

As an educator, your role is to model enthusiasm for all shared experiences and guide students in fostering mutual respect. By celebrating the diversity of their stories, you help students recognize the richness of their classroom community and the importance of valuing different perspectives.

Storytelling can be a transformative teaching tool that bridges cultural divides, fosters belonging, and encourages both individual and collective self-expression. Whether students are sharing their unique achievements or celebrating the values of their community, storytelling provides a platform for them to connect with their peers and find their voice in the classroom. When used thoughtfully, it strengthens the Teacher VIBE by ensuring every student feels valued, heard, and included.

Storifying Ideas That Benefit Collectivist Students and Modifications for Individualists

So what are some ways you can incorporate storytelling in your classroom? Figure 4.4 includes some storytelling (storifying) activities that benefit collectivist students, along with suggestions for how you can modify them to meet the needs of individualistic students.

Storytelling as a Bridge Between Cultures

Storytelling is a unique way to honor both individualistic and collectivist perspectives, fostering a classroom environment where every student feels seen and valued. Whether sharing personal victories or collective memories, storytelling enables students to bring their authentic selves into the learning experience.

By embracing both the "I" and the "we" (a concept explored further in "Why Empathy Matters in Teaching" in Chapter 6), educators create an inclusive and culturally responsive atmosphere where every story is respected. The Teacher VIBE requires approaching storytelling with an open heart and genuine appreciation for the diverse narratives that shape students' lives. This practice not only fosters belonging but also equips students

FIGURE 4.4
Storytelling Activities

Activity	Overview	Benefit to Collectivist Students	Modifications for Individualistic Students
Cultural storytelling circle	Students sit in a circle and share stories related to their cultural background, family history, or traditions, based on a theme introduced by the teacher.	It fosters community learning, active listening, and shared respect for stories, aligning with collectivist values.	Allow students to choose personal themes, write their stories beforehand, and reflect on individual meaning.
Group story creation	Students work together to create a story, with each member contributing to different aspects of the story (writing, illustrating, narrating).	It encourages collaborative creativity, shared responsibility, and teamwork, reflecting collectivist principles.	Assign individual roles like lead writer, encourage spin-off stories, and recognize individual creativity.
Historical storytelling	Students research historical events and retell them as stories, performing narratives from the perspective of someone who lived through the event.	It promotes empathy through collective storytelling, group research, and understanding of historical narratives.	Allow focus on a specific figure, written monologues, or solo projects for personal expression.
Myth and legend creation	Students collaborate to create original myths or legends explaining phenomena, inspired by existing cultural myths.	It strengthens group creativity and highlights cultural traditions of collective storytelling.	Offer individuals the opportunity to create their own myth, allow lead roles in storytelling, and give personal feedback on contributions.

(continued)

FIGURE 4.4
Storytelling Activities (*Continued*)

Activity	Overview	Benefit to Collectivist Students	Modifications for Individualistic Students
Peer story exchange	Students pair up to share and then retell each other's personal stories, incorporating important details or changes they feel are significant.	It builds peer connections, encourages empathy, and reinforces the importance of shared experiences.	Let students select significant personal stories, add personal flair, and reflect on the storytelling process.
Narrative-based problem solving	Students collaboratively solve a real-world problem presented as a story, creating a narrative solution as a group.	It promotes teamwork, encourages collective problem solving, and emphasizes solutions to benefit the community.	Allow individual narrative solutions, leadership roles in presenting solutions, and personal reflections on contribution.
Digital storytelling	Students work together to create a digital story using multimedia tools, combining different media into a cohesive project.	It encourages collaboration, emphasizes shared digital creation, and fosters unity in producing a meaningful project.	Assign specific roles, allow for solo digital stories, and recognize strong individual contributions.
Story-based debates	Students develop narrative resolutions to an unresolved story conflict or ethical dilemma and debate their chosen solution.	They promote group discussion, collective problem solving, and shared decision making.	Let students propose solo solutions, lead the debate, and reflect on their unique argumentation.

with the confidence, empathy, and understanding they need to navigate the world successfully (Qarooni, 2024).

Gamification in the Classroom: Blending Play and Learning

Growing up in the Nintendo era made me an avid gamer, and although my gaming time is now limited, I still enjoy occasional video-game nights with my kids. When I think of "gamification," I'm naturally drawn to memories of classics like *Super Mario Bros.* or *Minecraft*. These games are filled with badges, levels, boss battles, and upgrades, all designed to keep players motivated. But how do these gaming principles translate into education, and how can they enhance your Teacher VIBE?

What Is Gamification?

Gamification involves integrating game-inspired elements into educational settings to increase motivation and engagement (Haiken, 2017). Think of components like earning points, leveling up, unlocking badges, or completing quests. Although learning platforms like Kahoot! or interactive clicker systems are excellent tools for engagement, they are better categorized as *game-based learning*. Gamification goes beyond this categorization by creating an overarching storyline that ties lessons into a cohesive, immersive experience (Haiken, 2017).

For instance, imagine framing the school year as an epic adventure, where students take on roles as explorers working toward a grand mission. Each unit could present a new challenge, such as advocating for social justice or solving real-world problems. Students earn points, level up, and unlock rewards as they progress. The teacher becomes the "game master," dynamically adapting the adventure based on student input and progress.

Gamification and Belonging

Gamification can foster a sense of belonging by celebrating individual strengths, diverse backgrounds, and different ways of processing and engaging with information. In many games, players adopt *avatars*, or graphical representations of themselves (Christopoulos & Mystakidis, 2023), which can symbolize different roles such as the Warrior (achievement-driven), the Healer (collaborative and supportive), or the Wizard (innovative and strategic).

This concept directly aligns with the Teacher LENS framework discussed at length in Chapter 3. By observing students' behaviors early in the year, you can identify their learning avatars, helping you design gamified experiences that reflect their unique personalities and abilities. Let's explore some common avatar types found in role-playing games (RPGs) and how they might manifest in your students.

Using Your LENS to Identify Student Avatars

Each of the character avatars in RPGs—such as Warrior, Healer, or Wizard—has its own unique abilities and "playstyles." These avatars give players a way to engage with the game world in a manner that aligns with their personalities and strengths. As I describe some of these archetypal roles (see Figure 4.5), you may begin to identify your students as having these same diverse characteristics, preferences, and ways of engaging with and making sense of the learning process. Using the LENS framework to recognize these traits in students, you can create more tailored and effective learning environments. Additionally, understanding whether students lean more toward individualistic or collectivist behaviors can help in designing learning experiences that resonate with their cultural and personal inclinations.

FIGURE 4.5
Avatars and Suggested Supports

Avatar	LENS (Observation)	Individualist or Collectivist	Suggested Supports
Warrior	Takes charge, leads groups, seeks challenges	Individualistic	Assign leadership roles in group projects and offer challenging tasks that push their limits.
Healer	Helps others, focuses on group success, supports from the background	Collectivist	Provide opportunities for peer tutoring or supportive roles in group tasks. Acknowledge their contributions to group success.
Wizard	Is independent, analytical, a problem solver	Individualistic	Give open-ended projects and allow time for independent research. Encourage them to share creative solutions with the class.
Rogue	Prefers working alone, is efficient, self-motivated	Individualistic	Assign individual projects and give them autonomy in how they approach tasks. Let them work at their own pace.
Archer	Is detail-oriented, patient, methodical	Individualistic	Provide tasks that reward attention to detail, such as science experiments or research projects. Allow extra time for planning.
Paladin	Balances leadership and support, is empathetic	Hybrid (Individualistic and Collectivist)	Alternate between giving leadership and supportive roles in group projects. Encourage them to mentor classmates.

(continued)

FIGURE 4.5
Avatars and Suggested Supports (*Continued*)

Avatar	LENS (Observation)	Individualist or Collectivist	Suggested Supports
Bard	Is social, creative, enjoys connecting people	Collectivist	Assign creative, artistic projects or presentations. Encourage them to help connect group ideas and foster collaboration.
Druid	Is versatile, adapts to different roles, is nature-focused	Collectivist	Allow them to take on multiple roles in projects and offer nature- or environment-based tasks. Provide flexibility in assignments.

Let's start with exploring common RPG avatars and how they align with different student characteristics. The Warrior, for example, is a strong, durable fighter who thrives in leadership roles and enjoys challenges (Ahmad & Law, 2021). Students who display Warrior traits in the classroom are often confident, assertive, and willing to take charge during group activities or discussions. They enjoy responsibility and tend to lead their peers and look for recognition for their efforts.

The Healer, on the other hand, is a more team-oriented and empathetic individual. Healers focus on supporting others and ensuring harmony within the group (Ahmad & Law, 2021). In the classroom, these students may quietly help their classmates, offer guidance, and prefer cooperative roles where they can uplift others rather than stand out on their own.

The Wizard is the strategist who uses creativity and intelligence to solve problems (Peterson, 2020). Wizards in the classroom prefer working independently and excel in complex, abstract thinking tasks. They often contribute innovative ideas or solutions but may prefer to work alone rather than in groups.

Similarly, the Rogue is another independent avatar, preferring to work in the background with efficiency and stealth (Craddock, 2021). Students who align with the Rogue archetype are your independent workers who often prefer individual assignments, working quickly and resourcefully without the need for much guidance.

Then there's the Archer, a precision-focused character who values accuracy and patience (Peterson, 2020). In class, these students are your perfectionists, excelling at tasks requiring detailed attention, such as science experiments or math problems. They can easily remember formulas, are methodical, and prefer careful planning before acting.

The Paladin is a hybrid of leadership and support, balancing the desire to lead with a deep concern for the group's moral (Peterson, 2020). Students with Paladin traits will step up to lead when necessary but will also accept supportive roles as long as the group succeeds.

Creative students may align with the Bard, a social and artistic role that does extremely well connecting others (Peterson, 2020). Bards in the classroom enjoy using creativity, whether in writing, art, or music, to inspire their classmates. Additionally, they often act as the glue in group projects, fostering cohesion and creativity.

Finally, the Druid is adaptable and connected to nature, often excelling in environmental or interdisciplinary projects (Peterson, 2020). Druids are versatile students who can switch between roles as needed, contributing wherever they're most useful. Consider them the role-players that can do a bit of everything.

If you use your LENS, you can identify these avatar-like traits in students through careful observation of how they approach tasks and interact with each other. For example, Warriors naturally take charge in group work, whereas Rogues may prefer working alone. Wizards will gravitate toward problem-solving challenges, and Healers will quietly support their classmates. Understanding these tendencies gives you what you need to create culturally responsive gamified experiences according to students' strengths and preferences. Figure 4.6 summarizes the key strengths and potential roles of the various avatars.

FIGURE 4.6
Avatars and Their Key Strengths

Avatar	Key Strengths	How to Use This in Class
Warrior	Leadership, confidence, take-charge orientation	Lead group projects; handle challenging tasks; help guide others.
Healer	Empathy, team orientation, supportiveness	Help classmates; support group dynamics; focus on teamwork.
Wizard	Creativity, problem-solving ability, independence	Work on creative, independent tasks; share ideas with the class.
Rogue	Independence, efficiency, resourcefulness	Handle individual tasks; work quietly and efficiently.
Archer	Detail orientation, patience, carefulness	Excel in tasks requiring precision; help keep group projects organized.
Paladin	Balance between leadership and helper role	Lead when needed but also support the group; combine leadership and empathy.
Bard	Creativity, sociability, pleasure in connecting people	Use creativity to inspire others, make projects more enjoyable, and connect the team.
Druid	Adaptability, flexibility, versatility	Switch roles as needed to support the group and ensure success in dynamic environments.

Beyond identifying these traits, it's also essential to recognize whether a student's archetypes lean more toward individualistic or collectivist tendencies. Students who are more individualistic will align with avatars like the Warrior, Wizard, Rogue, or Archer, preferring to work alone, take the lead, or showcase their unique strengths. These avatars enjoy personal recognition and thrive in environments where they can take ownership of their tasks.

Conversely, collectivist students will align more closely with avatars like the Healer, Paladin, Bard, and Druid. These students excel in the role of helping others and contributing to the collective success of the team. They may not seek the spotlight but instead find satisfaction in ensuring that the group functions well as a whole.

With that being said, some avatars, such as the Paladin and the Wizard, can display both individualistic and collectivist traits, depending on the context. For example, Paladins balance leadership and support, making them adaptable to either group or individual roles. You can use their flexible style to your advantage when you need to balance teams. Wizards may prefer independent work but can also contribute valuable strategic insights in group settings when needed as well.

The avatars we see in video games offer a helpful framework for understanding the diverse strengths and preferences students bring to the classroom. Whether a student is a Warrior who seeks leadership and recognition or a Healer who prefers to support others, using the LENS to identify these traits allows you to personalize your approach and create a more engaging, dynamic learning experience for every type of learner.

First-Day Activity: What's Your Classroom Avatar?

The following activity is designed to help your students discover their avatar.

Find Out Which Video Game Character Matches Your Strengths

In video games, characters play different roles—some lead, others help, and some work alone to solve puzzles. Just like in games, every student learns and works in their own way. This activity will help you find out which video game character is most like YOU in the classroom!

How to Do This Activity

Answer the following questions honestly. Circle the answer that fits you best. At the end, you'll learn which character matches your strengths and how to use those strengths in school.

Part 1: How Do You Like to Do Schoolwork?

1. When you're in a group project, you . . .
    - A. Take charge and make sure everyone has a job.
    - B. Help everyone get along and pitch in where needed.
    - C. Work on the hardest part by yourself.
    - D. Do your part quickly and stay behind the scenes.
    - E. Focus on making everything perfect, even if it takes extra time.
    - F. Lead when needed but also support others.
    - G. Share creative ideas or try to make the group more fun.
    - H. Do whatever the group needs most to succeed.

2. When there's a tough challenge in class, you . . .
    A. Jump in and face it head-on.
    B. Help others figure it out.
    C. Think of different solutions on your own.
    D. Solve it quickly and quietly.
    E. Plan carefully and make sure everything is right.
    F. Lead and support the team at the same time.
    G. Offer creative ways to solve the problem.
    H. Adapt and take on the role that's needed.
3. In a group setting, you prefer to . . .
    A. Be the leader and keep things organized.
    B. Help others and check in on everyone.
    C. Come up with ideas and strategies.
    D. Work quietly on your part but still help the team.
    E. Make sure everything looks and works perfectly.
    F. Balance leading and helping.
    G. Use creativity to make the group work better.
    H. Change roles as needed to support the group.
4. When working on a creative project, you . . .
    A. Lead the brainstorming and assign parts to everyone.
    B. Help the group by doing whatever is needed.
    C. Think of cool new ideas or ways to do things.
    D. Focus on your part and get it done quickly.
    E. Make sure everything is just right and polished.
    F. Help the team while also guiding them when needed.
    G. Make the project more fun and exciting for everyone.
    H. Adjust to whatever the group needs to do well.

(continued)

Part 2: What Motivates You?
  5. What makes you feel proud?
     A. Leading a group or being recognized for doing well.
     B. Helping others and seeing the group succeed.
     C. Solving a hard problem or coming up with a great idea.
     D. Finishing my work quickly and well.
     E. Knowing I worked hard and got all the details right.
     F. Being a leader while also supporting the team.
     G. Making a project more creative or fun.
     H. Adapting to help the team when they need it.
  6. What kind of tasks do you like best?
     A. Tasks where I can lead and make decisions.
     B. Tasks where I can help others in a team.
     C. Independent tasks that let me solve problems or be creative.
     D. Quick tasks I can do on my own.
     E. Tasks that require careful planning and details.
     F. Tasks where I can lead and help equally.
     G. Creative tasks that make work more fun.
     H. Tasks where I can adapt and switch roles.

Part 3: Your Avatar Traits
  7. Which of these descriptions fits you best?
     A. I'm a leader who likes to take charge.
     B. I'm a helper who makes sure everyone's OK.
     C. I'm a thinker who solves problems and creates ideas.
     D. I'm independent and like working alone.
     E. I'm detail-oriented and careful.
     F. I'm balanced between leading and helping.

G. I'm creative and love making things fun.
H. I'm flexible and adapt to what the group needs.
8. When things get hard, I . . .
    A. Face the challenge head-on.
    B. Help others, even if it's hard for me, too.
    C. Think through how to solve it on my own.
    D. Push through quickly and move on.
    E. Take my time to make sure everything is done right.
    F. Help the group while also leading if needed.
    G. Add creativity or fun to make it better.
    H. Do whatever is needed to help the group.

Scoring: What's Your Avatar?
- Mostly As: You're a Warrior! A strong leader who takes charge.
- Mostly Bs: You're a Healer! Great at helping and supporting others.
- Mostly Cs: You're a Wizard! Creative and smart, solving problems on your own.
- Mostly Ds: You're a Rogue! Independent and efficient.
- Mostly Es: You're an Archer! Focused on details and precision.
- Mostly Fs: You're a Paladin! Balanced between leading and helping.
- Mostly Gs: You're a Bard! Fun and creative, bringing joy to the group.
- Mostly Hs: You're a Druid! Flexible and adaptable.

Reflection: How to Use Your Avatar
Now that you know your classroom avatar, think about how you can use your strengths to succeed. Share your avatar with your teacher and see how you can shine in group projects, assignments, and class activities!

Support for Both Individualistic and Collectivist Cultures

One of the strengths of gamification is its flexibility in supporting both individualistic and collectivist cultures. Gamification supports individualistic students by offering solo quests or chances for students to earn points through their own accomplishments. A student might complete an individual task to earn extra points or unlock a classroom privilege. On the other hand, collectivist students work together to solve problems or defeat "bosses" in group challenges, such as "boss battles" where students team up to tackle tough tasks or solve complex problems, pooling their skills to succeed. This type of collaboration strengthens a sense of belonging, making it easier for students from collectivist cultures to fully engage with the learning experience. By offering both individual tasks and group challenges, gamified classrooms can appeal to students from a variety of cultural backgrounds, ensuring that everyone feels included and motivated.

A Way to Redefine Failure

One of the most valuable aspects of gamification is how it changes the way students view failure. In a traditional classroom, failing a test or an assignment can feel like the end of the road for some students, especially for students who struggle with confidence. But in a gamified classroom, failure is just part of the process—as in a video game, where players often fail multiple times before finally attaining a higher level. Therefore, students who might normally give up after receiving a bad grade are more likely to keep trying in a gamified setting. The possibility of earning points, leveling up, or unlocking rewards keeps them motivated and focused, helping them see failure as a stepping stone to success.

How to Get Started with Gamifying Your Classroom

If you're new to gamification, the prospect of incorporating it into your classroom routine might seem overwhelming, especially if you don't have experience playing video games yourself. Your skills will develop over time, however. Here's how to ease into it:

- **Start small.** Try gamifying a single lesson or unit to begin with. Choose a lesson that could benefit from competition or teamwork, and add in simple elements like points, badges, or a mission for students to complete by the end.
- **Call in your gamers.** I can guarantee that your class has students who are already into gaming. Use their knowledge to help shape your gamified classroom. Ask them for ideas on how to structure challenges or make the experience more engaging.
- **Focus on storytelling.** Once you're comfortable, you can add a storyline that spans a whole unit or even the school year. You can build this storyline around your students' interests, like a popular video game, a TV show, or a book. Incorporating a storyline gives students a reason to stay engaged with their learning.
- **Offer choices.** One of the biggest benefits of gamification is letting students have a say in how they learn. Whether it's choosing an avatar, deciding which missions to tackle, or opting to work alone or in groups, giving students options boosts their engagement.
- **Separate game points from grades.** Keep game points and academic grades separate. In a gamified classroom, game points unlock rewards or powers in the classroom but

don't replace traditional grading. This distinction ensures that academic assessment remains fair and standards-based, while game points add an extra layer of fun and motivation.

The Power of Play

Gamification can add an additional layer of fun to your classroom community. By embedding game-like elements, you can create environments that make students eager to participate, collaborate, and persevere. Whether it's through individual tasks like leveling up or group challenges like boss battles, gamification has something for every type of learner.

Remember to start small; you don't have to go all in at once. Start small, build from there, and make sure it's enjoyable for both you and your students. After all, learning should be fun!

Gamification Ideas for Collectivist and Individualistic Students

Shifting away from traditional teaching approaches, which rely heavily on individualistic norms, gamification can be highly effective for engaging all students by turning learning into a dynamic, interactive experience. For collectivist students, gamifying learning activities can foster collaboration, community involvement, and shared goals, aligning with their cultural values. Additionally, you can modify these activities to meet the needs of your individualistic students, who may prefer competition, personal recognition, and autonomy in their learning. Figure 4.7 includes several ideas for gamified learning that can benefit collectivist students, along with suggestions for modifications to accommodate individualistic students.

FIGURE 4.7
Types of Game-Based Activities for Collectivists, with Modifications for Individualists

Activity	Overview	Benefits for Collectivist Students	Modifications for Individualistic Students
Team-based challenges and competitions	Divide the class into teams to complete tasks like solving math problems or participating in quizzes. Teams earn points and unlock rewards as they progress.	• They encourage teamwork and shared responsibility. • They focus on group success and problem solving.	• Allow personal achievements within the team (e.g., "Best Problem Solver"). • Offer individual recognition alongside group rewards. • Provide leadership roles.
Classroom leaderboards with team goals	Teams earn points by completing tasks, with a leaderboard tracking progress. Rewards are given when milestones are reached.	• They promote unity and shared progress. • They emphasize collaboration over individual competition.	• Include individual leaderboards for personal progress. • Offer badges for individual accomplishments. • Allow personal milestones.
Escape room–style learning	Students work together to solve puzzles and unlock clues to "escape" the room. Could be used for various subjects.	• It encourages cooperation and interdependence. • It relies on group effort to succeed.	• Assign specific roles like "Code Cracker." • Provide solo challenges within the game. • Recognize individual achievements.
Classroom quest games	Students form groups or "guilds" to complete academic tasks and gain experience points (XPs), advancing through levels in an ongoing classroom adventure.	• They promote long-term collaboration and shared experiences. • They foster group cohesion and collective achievement.	• Allow individual students to earn XPs for side quests. • Offer leadership roles like "guild leader." • Provide individual rewards.

(continued)

FIGURE 4.7
Types of Game-Based Activities for Collectivists, with Modifications for Individualists (*Continued*)

Activity	Overview	Benefits for Collectivist Students	Modifications for Individualistic Students
Interactive learning platforms (Kahoot!, Quizizz, etc.)	Use platforms like Kahoot! to participate in real-time quizzes as a team, earning points for correct answers.	• They foster teamwork and reduce pressure on individuals. • They focus on group performance and success.	• Include individual scores alongside team scores. • Offer awards for top scorers. • Let students create and lead quizzes.
Classroom economy or reward system	Create a point-based system that enables students to earn "classroom currency" for completing tasks, which they can spend on privileges or rewards.	• It encourages collective effort to earn rewards. • It promotes shared responsibility and success.	• Allow students to earn personal currency. • Create individual challenges for extra currency. • Recognize top earners individually.
Role-playing and simulation games	Students take on roles in scenarios (e.g., running a business or managing a town) and work together to solve problems and make decisions.	• They promote group decision making and cooperation. • They build community through shared experiences.	• Assign leadership roles like "CEO" or "mayor." • Offer solo decision-making tasks that affect the group. • Recognize leadership and creative solutions.
Badge and achievement systems	Implement a system where students earn badges for completing tasks, mastering skills, or contributing to group projects.	• They encourage shared effort to earn badges as a team. • They foster collective pride in team achievements.	• Offer individual badges for personal goals. • Let students customize their badges. • Track personal milestones for individual progress.

Summing Up and Looking Ahead

Much like *The Legend of Zelda* revolutionized gaming by allowing players to save their progress and engage with the game over time, today's educators can transform the classroom into a collective, shared learning experience. Decolonize your classroom by moving away from Western modes of Eurocentrism and focusing on recovering "alternative" or non-Eurocentric ways of knowing (Eakins, 2022). Moving away from a traditional, individualistic approach toward a more collaborative, community-focused model encourages students to learn together, support one another, and build on their collective knowledge and strengths. This shift is crucial in creating a classroom environment where each student feels like a valuable member of the community.

In this chapter, I presented three key teaching practices that harness a collective approach to learning: project-based learning, storytelling, and gamification. These strategies offer powerful tools to foster a sense of belonging and collaboration in your classroom. Project-based learning connects students with real-world problems, encouraging them to work together, apply their cultural and individual strengths, and create meaningful projects that relate to their lived experiences. By using storytelling, students from both individualistic and collectivist cultures can share their unique narratives, bridging cultural gaps and deepening empathy within the classroom. Gamification, with its ability to appeal to different ways of engaging with content and diverse personalities, adds another layer of engagement, turning learning into a fun, interactive adventure that promotes both individual achievement and group success.

Finally, embracing these innovative approaches to teaching allows you to cultivate a student-centered classroom that reflects the diverse needs, interests, and strengths of each student. Like *Zelda's* golden cartridge, which stood out and symbolized a shift in gaming, these strategies represent a shift in education toward a greater emphasis on Valuing Inclusion and Belonging for Everyone. As you continue to build your Teacher VIBE, remember that the power of collective learning lies in our ability to engage, inspire, and connect with every student, ensuring that no one is left behind in the journey of discovery and growth.

In the next chapter, I'll focus on peer assessments as a tool for enhancing collectivist teaching. After discussing various activities and strategies in the previous chapters, we'll now explore ways to grade and assess projects, assignments, and presentations collaboratively. Peer assessments allow students to evaluate their classmates' work and provide feedback, promoting engagement, active learning, and critical-thinking skills.

5

Boosting Learning with Peer Assessments

As a kid, few classroom moments filled me with more dread than hearing the teacher say, "OK, we're going to swap papers and grade each other's work." My stomach would sink instantly—not because I didn't try or care about my work, but because of the vulnerability the statement brought. Having a peer—especially one I admired—see my mistakes felt like torture.

I vividly remember one particular instance in 5th grade. My crush, Sonia, and I were paired for grading each other's math tests. My heart raced as she began marking my rushed, unchecked answers. When she handed my paper back, her quick glance told me everything I didn't want to know. I spent the rest of the day embarrassed and overthinking the situation.

Looking back, this practice of swapping papers wasn't uncommon, but it taught little beyond identifying right and wrong answers. For many students, it served only as a source of embarrassment. Although teachers often used this practice to save time, it fell short of fostering meaningful learning or growth.

True peer assessment is much more than grading. It's about constructive feedback, thoughtful evaluation, and supporting one another's development. In this chapter, we'll explore the differences between peer grading and peer assessment, why the latter matters, and strategies to make it a positive and culturally responsive part of your classroom.

Peer Assessment Versus Peer Grading: How Embarrassment Affects Students

Having students swap papers for grading, although practical for teachers, often does more harm than good for students. It emphasizes judgment over growth and places students in uncomfortable positions. For those sensitive about peer perceptions, this practice can lead to stress and embarrassment, discouraging participation and risk taking in the classroom. For example, a student receiving a low grade in front of classmates may feel exposed, leading to a fear of making mistakes and diminished confidence. Although this method may save teachers time, it offers little educational value for students beyond marking answers.

Peer assessment, on the other hand, shifts the focus from *judgment* to *support*. It emphasizes growth, mutual respect, and constructive feedback. Instead of merely identifying errors, students learn to guide their peers toward improvement, fostering a classroom culture of empathy and collaboration.

When integrated thoughtfully, peer assessment aligns with the Teacher VIBE. It's a student-centered approach that prioritizes inclusion and belonging. It empowers students to take ownership of their learning while helping their peers do the same.

What Is Peer Assessment, and Why Is It Beneficial?

Peer assessment is an educational approach in which students evaluate each other's work with the goal of providing constructive feedback and fostering growth (Sackstein, 2024). Unlike peer grading, which centers on right or wrong answers, peer assessment encourages students to do the following:

- Identify strengths in their peers' work.
- Offer thoughtful suggestions for improvement.
- Ask questions to clarify ideas or expand understanding.

The foundation of effective peer assessment is *trust*. Students must feel safe in sharing their work and give honest, respectful feedback. Building this trust requires a classroom culture that values openness, mutual respect, and a focus on growth rather than criticism.

Peer assessment is a powerful way to support students' growth while fostering a classroom culture that values both individual and collective success. When designed with cultural responsiveness, peer assessment creates opportunities for students to engage meaningfully with their learning and their peers. It benefits both collectivist and individualistic students in various ways.

For collectivist students, peer assessment does the following:

- **Builds connection.** Peer assessments enable collectivist students to collaborate and support their peers, fostering a sense of community and shared purpose.

- **Encourages respect.** By engaging with different perspectives, collectivist students learn to value and trust the contributions of their classmates.
- **Improves social and communication skills.** Through structured feedback, collectivist students practice active listening, constructive dialogue, and teamwork, strengthening their ability to work effectively in groups.
- **Supports the classroom community.** Collectivist students may feel more at ease receiving feedback from peers, promoting a more supportive and inclusive learning environment.

For individualistic students, peer assessment does the following:

- **Encourages self-reflection.** Peer assessment allows individualistic students to evaluate their own strengths and areas for improvement, supporting personal growth.
- **Builds critical-thinking skills.** Analyzing and providing feedback on peers' work sharpens their ability to think critically and evaluate quality in their own work.
- **Strengthens responsibility.** Peer assessment nurtures accountability by emphasizing the importance of both individual contributions and group collaboration.
- **Provides new ideas.** Observing how others approach a task broadens individualistic students' perspective, sparking inspiration for their own work.

All students benefit from peer assessment, as it contributes to desirable outcomes by doing the following:

- **Reinforces concepts.** Assessing peers' work deepens understanding and retention of key concepts. Teaching others is one of the best ways to learn.

- **Builds confidence and empathy.** Giving and receiving constructive feedback builds self-assurance while fostering empathy and mutual respect.
- **Blends cultural preferences.** By combining individual accountability with collaborative interaction, peer assessment creates a balanced approach that benefits all students.

Examples of Peer Assessment Activities

Peer assessment creates opportunities for students to engage meaningfully with their peers while respecting their individual and cultural preferences. The following are examples of how peer assessment can be used at various grade levels, along with specific benefits for collectivist and individualistic students.

Art Critique Circle in Mr. Driver's 3rd Grade Class

Activity: Students display their artwork in a "gallery" format around the room. Each student writes a positive note on at least two classmates' work, focusing on effort, creativity, or technique.

- **For collectivist students**, this activity fosters a sense of community and appreciation, as they celebrate each other's creativity and efforts.
- **For individualistic students**, observing diverse artistic styles inspires them to reflect on their own work and explore new ideas.

By encouraging both personal reflection and group appreciation, this activity supports a culture where creativity and individuality thrive within a collaborative framework.

Peer Review of a Writing Assignment in Ms. Patel's 5th Grade Class

Activity: Students exchange writing assignments and provide feedback, highlighting strengths and suggesting one area for improvement.

- **For collectivist students**, the peer review process creates a collaborative and supportive space where they feel valued and connected.
- **For individualistic students**, reviewing others' writing encourages them to think critically and gain insights to improve their own work.

Ms. Patel's peer review activity helps students build confidence, hone their skills, and create a classroom culture of growth and respect.

Reflection on an Experiment in Mr. Kline's 8th Grade Science Class

Activity: After completing a lab experiment, students pair up to review each other's lab reports, offering feedback on clarity, accuracy, and conclusions.

- **For collectivist students**, collaborating on reviews of lab reports allows them to support one another's understanding of scientific concepts while working toward shared goals.
- **For individualistic students**, analyzing peers' reports helps them reflect on their own reasoning and improve their ability to present findings clearly.

This peer reflection reinforces the idea that every student's effort contributes to the collective success of the group while enhancing individual learning.

What the Examples Demonstrate

The examples just described show how peer assessment functions as an essential tool for cultivating a supportive classroom community that honors both individual achievements and collective growth. By implementing culturally responsive peer assessment practices, you can create a classroom environment where students feel valued, empowered, and connected. The activities described here provide opportunities for students to grow academically and socially while reinforcing the Teacher VIBE of inclusion and belonging for everyone.

Setting Up Peer Assessment: Teaching Students How to Give Feedback

As with any other teaching strategy discussed in this book, establishing peer assessment in your classroom requires intentional preparation. Peer assessment is more than just students exchanging papers and providing feedback. It's about cultivating trust, connection, and a collective learning experience.

Begin by explaining the purpose of peer assessment to your students. Emphasize that it's not solely about identifying strengths and weaknesses but about fostering a supportive classroom community where everyone plays a role in each other's growth.

Introduce feedback as a powerful tool to support learning, where every student's voice matters. Align this with your Teacher VIBE, ensuring a student-centered focus by discussing the importance of mutual support in their educational journey. Start with a whole-class lesson to model examples of both positive and constructive feedback. Highlight the use of respectful and specific language that appreciates effort and offers actionable suggestions to improve.

Teach Glow and Grow

A great starting point for teaching feedback is introducing the concept of Glow and Grow. Explain what students will be expected to do, as suggested by these two words:

- **Glow:** Highlight the strengths of the work.
- **Grow:** Suggest areas for improvement in a constructive and supportive way.

This simple framework helps students understand that feedback is a balanced mix of encouragement and helpful guidance.

Begin by teaching students to use structured feedback stems, such as these:

- "One thing I liked was..."
- "You could make it even better by..."

These stems encourage students to provide meaningful, balanced feedback, and they make the process less intimidating.

How to Make a Positive Sandwich

Teach students to use the Positive Sandwich method, which starts with a positive comment, followed by a constructive suggestion, and ends with another positive comment. This strategy adds another layer to the Glow and Grow structure, making constructive feedback feel less critical and more balanced.

Start Small and Build Confidence

Incorporate these strategies into simple, low-pressure activities—what I like to call "low-hanging fruit." These can be activities that are familiar or straightforward, like reviewing anonymous work samples or examples you provide. This approach helps students practice giving feedback without the added pressure of critiquing a peer's personal work right away.

Encourage students to work in pairs or small groups to discuss their feedback, reinforcing the importance of collaboration and mutual respect. Doing so allows them to practice the following skills:

- Observing and identifying strengths in others' work.
- Communicating suggestions in a way that feels safe and nonjudgmental.
- Actively listening and responding thoughtfully.

As students become more comfortable with the process, gradually transition to having them assess their peers' actual work.

VIBE-Aligned Feedback Stems That Support Belonging and Respect

As our classroom demographics continue to change, culturally responsive feedback is essential for creating a sense of belonging in your students. As mentioned before, developing peer assessment protocols for your students includes modeling ways to provide feedback that is meaningful to peers. In this section, I will discuss ways to teach students how to give feedback through feedback stems. These stems help students learn to give meaningful, respectful, and supportive feedback that honors the unique backgrounds and perspectives of their classmates. You may find that eventually they won't need to use the stems and can give feedback on their own.

Ultimately, culturally responsive feedback stems create a classroom environment where all students—regardless of their cultural background—have a sense of belonging. By teaching students to use these stems, you empower your students to engage in constructive dialogue, develop empathy, and strengthen the bonds in your classroom community. These stems support the following desirable behaviors:

- **Encouraging respect for diverse perspectives.** The feedback stems are meant to encourage specific, respectful language that recognizes each student's unique approach. Phrases like "I loved how you . . ." and "Your work made me think of . . ." allow students to express appreciation for their peer's individual perspective.
- **Supporting inclusion and belonging.** The feedback stems incorporate language that supports a sense of community and inclusion. For example, stems such as "Your ideas made me want to learn more" or "The way you explained it helped me understand better" highlight genuine curiosity and openness, making students feel their contributions are valued.
- **Promoting growth mindset and mutual support.** The constructive feedback stems are framed in a way that encourages improvement without criticism, which is essential in culturally responsive settings. Suggestions like "Maybe you could add . . ." or "One way to make this stronger . . ." offer respectful guidance rather than judgment, supporting a growth mindset that is considerate of each student's background.
- **Providing specific, observable feedback.** Stems focus on specific, observable elements rather than subjective opinions. Culturally responsive feedback avoids generalized praise or critique and instead highlights an authentic approach to the work, making feedback feel respectful, clear, and constructive for all students.

Figure 5.1 presents examples of positive and constructive comments that incorporate feedback stems. Use these in a

FIGURE 5.1
Examples of Positive and Constructive Feedback

Elementary School	Middle School	High School
Positive Feedback Examples		
"I loved the colors you used; they made your work feel happy!"	"Your choice of colors made your work stand out and look bold."	"Your argument was clear and well-supported, and I liked your unique perspective."
"Your story was so fun to read, especially the part where [specific detail]."	"I liked how you organized your points clearly; it was easy to follow."	"The contrast and detail in your work brought out strong emotions."
"The way you explained your idea made it easy to understand."	"Your creativity really showed in the way you used [specific technique]."	"The way you explained each step made it easy to follow."
"I liked how you used expression when reading; it made the story come alive!"	"The visuals were helpful and made your ideas easier to understand."	"Your visuals helped communicate your ideas effectively."
"Your drawing had great details; it was exciting to look at!"	"Your steps were clear, and I understood each part."	"The examples you included made your points feel very relevant."
"Your ideas were creative, and I could picture what you described."	"I liked how you connected [topic] to real-world examples; it felt relevant."	"Connecting the topic to current events was a great touch; it felt relatable."
"I enjoyed how clear and neat your work was!"	"Your characters felt real, and I enjoyed the dialogue."	"Your voice was confident, and your points were well-organized."
"The examples you used helped me understand the idea better."	"The story had great details, which made it easy to picture."	"The character development was impressive; the characters felt real."
"The way you shared your thoughts made me want to learn more!"	"Your project was interesting, and I could see the effort you put in."	"Your explanation made me see the topic from a new perspective."
"I liked how you spoke loudly and clearly; it made it easy to follow."	"Your writing was engaging and kept my attention."	"Your research added depth and showed your dedication to understanding the topic."

(continued)

FIGURE 5.1
Examples of Positive and Constructive Feedback (*Continued*)

Elementary School	Middle School	High School
Constructive Feedback Examples		
"Maybe you could slow down a little so everyone can understand better."	"Maybe try adding more shading to give it a bit more depth and realism."	"Adding more evidence could make your argument even stronger."
"It might be even better if you added a little more detail to explain your ideas."	"Adding some background information could help explain your points even better."	"Experimenting with more texture could add visual interest."
"You could try adding more background details to make it look even cooler."	"It could help to slow down a bit on the important parts so we can understand them fully."	"Explaining your method a bit more could help clarify your thought process."
"To make it clearer, you might organize each step more neatly."	"Adding a few more details could make your argument even stronger."	"More real-world examples might strengthen your points even further."
"One way to make it even stronger is to double-check for small mistakes."	"Including sensory details could make the setting easier to picture."	"Adding additional research could back up your claims even more."
"Adding some more colors could make it stand out even more."	"You could add another example to make your explanation more complete."	"Breaking down the steps more could make it easier to follow."
"Try pausing a little between sentences when you read so everyone can keep up."	"Try organizing the slides a bit more so the flow is smoother."	"Expanding your conclusion might help tie everything together clearly."
"You might add a bit more about what happens next to complete the story."	"It might help if you explained why you chose this approach."	"Organizing your main points more could make the argument flow better."
"To make it easier to understand, you could add a couple of examples."	"Adding captions to your visuals could make them easier to follow."	"Including more data might make your findings even more convincing."
"Maybe try adding labels or captions to make it easier to follow."	"Try expanding your analysis to give more depth to your findings."	"Connecting to a broader context could add depth to your analysis."

whole-class format, where you as the teacher provide feedback and ask students to try their own. For instance, display a student's artwork or writing and ask the class to give "glow" and "grow" feedback.

While practicing with students, encourage them to make their feedback specific and observable. The stems are just guides and should never create a "copy and paste" type of feeling. Remind students that specific feedback is more meaningful and shows the student that their work was truly understood. Ask students questions like "How can you show your classmates that you observed details in their work?" Prompt students to comment on observable parts of their peer's work rather than personal opinions. For example, instead of "This looks boring," they might say, "You could add more colors to make it stand out."

After a few feedback sessions, guide students in reflecting on their experience by asking how they felt giving and receiving feedback. This reflection helps them understand the positive impact that constructive feedback can have and highlights areas where they can improve. Encourage a discussion on how feedback has contributed to their growth in the past. Developing an appreciation for the process and reinforcing that feedback is a natural and beneficial part of learning. This approach not only deepens their understanding of feedback's value but also normalizes it as a key component of their educational journey.

Throughout the setting up and training, reinforce the importance of empathy, framing feedback as an opportunity to encourage their classmates and contribute positively to their learning journey. Gradually shift to partner or group feedback sessions, ensuring that students reflect on both giving and receiving feedback to strengthen their understanding. Throughout this process, celebrate successes and reinforce the notion that constructive, specific feedback strengthens not just individual learning but the overall sense of belonging and support within the classroom community.

Here's an example of a set of steps to follow in introducing and implementing feedback activities:

1. **Introduction:** Explain the purpose of feedback and introduce the Glow and Grow concept.
2. **Modeling:** Demonstrate effective feedback using examples and respectful language.
3. **Feedback stems:** Go over feedback stems and practice them with sample work.
4. **Practicing the Positive Sandwich technique:** Teach the technique and practice with various examples.
5. **Small-group practice:** Divide students into groups for a feedback activity, using feedback stems and the Positive Sandwich.
6. **Reflection:** Discuss how it felt to give and receive feedback, reinforcing the idea that feedback is about growth and support.

Peer Assessment Strategies

Here are some of my favorite peer assessment strategies to use in the classroom, designed to "mix things up" and keep students engaged. Each strategy encourages different ways of giving feedback, allowing students to develop their communication skills and build a stronger sense of belonging within the classroom. You may find that students gravitate toward particular methods, developing their own favorites that resonate with their cultural values and preferred ways of engaging with learning. As a teacher, you can observe these preferences and incorporate the most effective or popular strategies more frequently, creating a feedback-rich environment that fosters growth, trust, and collaboration.

- **Two Stars and a Wish**
  - **What is it?** Students review a peer's work and give two positive comments (the "stars") and one constructive suggestion (the "wish").
  - **Objective:** This activity teaches students to balance positive and constructive feedback, using both "glow" and "grow" comments.
  - **Example:** After a writing or art project, pair students and have them use Two Stars and a Wish to review each other's work. You can use feedback stems to guide them.
- **Gallery Walk with Feedback Sticky Notes**
  - **What is it?** Display student work around the room, such as artwork, posters, or written projects. Students walk around, viewing each piece, and leave sticky notes with positive and constructive feedback.
  - **Objective:** This activity allows students to see a variety of work and give feedback anonymously, which can make them feel more comfortable.
  - **Example:** After a social studies or science project, conduct a gallery walk. Tell students to use feedback stems on sticky notes, leaving one positive and one constructive comment for at least three projects.
- **Peer Feedback Carousel**
  - **What is it?** Students form small groups and rotate between each group member's work, giving feedback at each "station."
  - **Objective:** The carousel setup provides students with multiple perspectives on their work and gives

each student a chance to practice giving feedback several times.
- **Example:** For a math problem-solving activity, students could solve a problem on a sheet, then pass it around the group, with each student adding feedback on clarity and solution strategy.

- **Feedback Bingo**
  - **What is it?** Create a bingo card with feedback prompts in each box (e.g., "I liked your use of details," "I wonder if you could add more examples," "Your explanation was clear"). Students fill out or circle boxes on a bingo card by providing feedback that matches the prompts.
  - **Objective:** Feedback Bingo introduces variety in feedback language and helps students practice giving feedback in a structured way.
  - **Example:** After a creative writing exercise, give students a bingo card with feedback prompts. As they read a peer's story, they select prompts from the card to complete a line or column, or they circle their feedback on the card.

- **Peer Feedback Role-Playing**
  - **What is it?** Divide students into pairs or small groups and give each student a "role" for the feedback session (e.g., Positivity Coach, Specifics Expert, or Growth Guide). Each student gives feedback based on their assigned role.
  - **Objective:** Role-playing encourages students to focus on different aspects of feedback, helping them see feedback from multiple angles.

- **Example:** After a science experiment or lab report, assign roles and have students give feedback in pairs. Positivity Coaches focus on positive comments, whereas Growth Guides offer constructive suggestions.
- **Feedback Ladder**
  - **What is it?** In this activity, students give feedback in stages. First, they give a general compliment, then identify a specific strength, and finally provide a constructive suggestion.
  - **Objective:** The "ladder" structure helps students move from positive to constructive feedback in a gentle and structured way.
  - **Example:** After a presentation, ask students to use the Feedback Ladder to review a peer's work. They might start with "I enjoyed your topic," then give a specific strength like "Your visuals were clear," and end with a suggestion like "You might slow down for important points."
- **Feedback Journal Exchange**
  - **What is it?** Each student keeps a journal or digital document where they receive and reflect on feedback. Peers leave feedback entries, and the recipient reflects on how they might use the feedback to improve.
  - **Objective:** A feedback journal allows students to track their growth and see feedback as part of their learning journey.
  - **Example:** For an ongoing project, have students exchange journals weekly with a partner, leaving

feedback on each entry. Each week, students reflect in their journal on how they're applying their partner's feedback.

- **Glow and Grow Circles**
  - **What is it?** Students sit in a circle and take turns sharing one "glow" (something they liked) and one "grow" (a suggestion for improvement) about a peer's work.
  - **Objective:** This activity encourages students to think carefully about both positive and constructive feedback, promoting a supportive classroom environment.
  - **Example:** After a class reading activity, form small circles and ask students to share a "glow" and a "grow" for a peer's reading expression and pacing.
- **Sentence-Starter Cards**
  - **What is it?** Each student receives a card with sentence starters for positive and constructive feedback (e.g., "One thing I liked was . . ." or "You might make it even better by . . ."). Students use these to give feedback during a partner activity.
  - **Objective:** Sentence starters give students language they can rely on, making feedback easier and more structured.
  - **Example:** After any group activity, distribute sentence-starter cards and have students provide feedback using the prompts.
- **Feedback Fishbowl**
  - **What is it?** A small group of students sits in the center of the room (the "fishbowl") and practices giving feedback on a sample piece of work. The rest

of the class observes, noting examples of strong feedback.
— **Objective:** This activity allows students to learn by observing, and the fishbowl participants get extra support in practicing feedback.
— **Example:** After a peer presents a story or project, choose a few students to give feedback in the fishbowl while the class observes. Rotate groups so all students experience both giving and observing feedback.

Examples of Peer Assessments Done Correctly

The preceding descriptions of peer assessment strategies suggest a number of ways to engage students in this activity. It's also useful to look at specific examples of correct implementation. Here are examples at various grade levels.

Middle school: Science experiment reflection in 7th grade

Context: After conducting a simple experiment on plant growth, students pair up to review each other's lab reports, using the Two Stars and a Wish method to provide feedback.

- **Positive feedback 1:** "Your results were organized really well, and it made it easy to understand the changes over time."
- **Positive feedback 2:** "I liked how you explained the impact of sunlight in your conclusion. It helped me see why it matters."
- **Constructive suggestion:** "You might try adding a little more detail about the different types of plants you used. That would make it easier for people to follow your experiment."

Why it's effective: This feedback acknowledges the student's strengths in organization and explanation, while suggesting an improvement that is specific and easily actionable. The feedback is respectful and focused on enhancing clarity, making it supportive and growth-oriented.

High school: English essay peer review in 10th grade

Context: After drafting a persuasive essay, students swap papers and use the Positive Sandwich technique to provide feedback. Each student offers one positive comment, a constructive suggestion, and a final positive comment.

- **First positive feedback:** "Your argument was really clear, and I liked your unique perspective on the topic. It made me think about it in a new way."
- **Constructive suggestion:** "To make your argument even stronger, you might add more evidence in the third paragraph to support your main point."
- **Final positive feedback:** "Your introduction was really engaging; it grabbed my attention right from the start."

Why it's effective: This feedback uses the Positive Sandwich to balance appreciation with constructive feedback. The student is praised for a clear argument and engaging introduction while being gently encouraged to strengthen their evidence in a specific part of the essay. This approach respects the writer's work and offers actionable guidance for improvement.

Elementary school: Reading aloud in 4th grade

Context: After a reading-aloud exercise, students are paired to provide feedback on expression, pacing, and clarity using a structured Glow and Grow format.

- **Glow:** "I liked how you used your voice to make the characters sound different; it made the story fun to listen to!"
- **Grow:** "Next time, you might try slowing down a little in the middle part so we can hear every word clearly."

Why it's effective: The feedback celebrates the student's expressive reading, which is a valuable skill, while offering a gentle suggestion to slow down for better clarity. It balances support with encouragement for growth in a way that is positive and constructive.

Middle school: Math problem solving in 6th grade

Context: After solving a challenging math problem, students pair up to compare their methods and provide feedback using the Feedback Ladder (general compliment → specific strength → constructive suggestion).

- **General compliment:** "I really liked how you solved the problem; it looked organized and neat."
- **Specific strength:** "The way you showed each step helped me understand your approach."
- **Constructive suggestion:** "Maybe you could add a few notes on why you chose that method so it's even easier to follow."

Why it's effective: This feedback acknowledges the student's organization and clarity while suggesting that adding explanatory notes could further enhance understanding. It encourages the student to reflect on their reasoning process without diminishing their effort.

Examples of Peer Assessments Done Incorrectly

Examples of correct implementation of peer assessment strategies provide one side of the story. Just as useful are examples of *incorrect* implementation. Here are examples at various grade levels.

Elementary school: Art critique in 3rd grade

Context: After a gallery walk, a student gives feedback on a peer's drawing.

Feedback: "Your drawing doesn't look very real. You should try harder next time."

What's wrong: This feedback is too vague and lacks specific details about what could be improved. It comes across as negative and doesn't offer any constructive suggestions.

How to improve: Instead, the student could say, "I liked the colors you used; they made your drawing stand out! Maybe next time you could add more details to make it look more real." This rephrased feedback includes both positive and constructive comments, making it more supportive and specific.

Middle school: Science lab report in 7th grade

Context: After reviewing a lab report, a student provides feedback on a peer's experiment.

Feedback: "This doesn't make sense. You should rewrite it."

What's wrong: This feedback is too blunt and doesn't specify what part of the report is confusing. It also fails to provide any suggestions for improvement, leaving the student unsure of what to work on.

How to improve: The student could say, "I liked how you organized your results; it made the data easy to follow. To make it even clearer, you could add a sentence explaining why you think the experiment turned out this way." This alternative feedback is specific, is polite, and includes a constructive suggestion.

High school: Essay peer review in 10th grade

Context: Students swap essays for peer review. One student gives the following feedback.

Feedback: "Your argument is weak, and it was hard to follow."

What's wrong: This feedback is critical without being constructive. It's vague and lacks specific points that could help the student improve their argument.

How to improve: The feedback could be rephrased to say this: "I liked your introduction; it really caught my attention. To make your argument stronger, you might add more examples in the third paragraph to support your main point." This approach is more encouraging, is specific, and offers a clear path for improvement.

Elementary school: Reading aloud in 4th grade

Context: After a reading-aloud activity, a student gives feedback on a peer's reading.

Feedback: "You read too fast and didn't sound very good."

What's wrong: This feedback is overly critical and doesn't offer any specific advice. It may discourage the student and doesn't suggest how they could improve their reading skills.

How to improve: The student could say, "I liked how you used a lot of expression; it made the story interesting. Maybe next time you could slow down a little so we can hear every word clearly." This version is specific, is kind, and encourages growth without being harsh.

Middle school: Math problem solving in 6th grade

Context: After solving math problems in pairs, one student provides feedback on their partner's solution.

Feedback: "Your answer is wrong; you need to redo it."

What's wrong: This feedback is unhelpful because it's only focused on what's "wrong" without explaining why or how to fix it. It's dismissive and doesn't guide the student toward understanding their error.

How to improve: Instead, the student could say, "I noticed you worked hard on solving the problem. Maybe we could go over the steps together to see which step led you to an incorrect answer." This feedback acknowledges the effort, suggests collaboration, and avoids assigning blame, making it more supportive and constructive.

Some Challenges of Peer Assessments and Solutions

Peer assessment is a valuable tool for fostering collaborative learning, empathy, and critical thinking, but it also presents unique challenges that can affect students' sense of belonging. When students feel valued, respected, and supported, they are more likely to give and receive feedback effectively. However, issues like bias, vague feedback, fear of offending peers, or discomfort with constructive criticism can make students feel disconnected or uncertain, reducing the effectiveness of peer assessments. By addressing these challenges using your Teacher LENS, you can create a supportive environment where students see peer assessment as an opportunity to grow together. Figure 5.2 outlines common challenges and culturally responsive solutions to help teachers guide students in providing honest, constructive feedback that strengthens their relationships, promotes mutual respect, and fosters a connected, inclusive classroom.

FIGURE 5.2
Challenge-LENS-Solution

Challenge	LENS	Solution
Bias and favoritism	Bias can make some students feel excluded or undervalued, creating divides in the classroom.	Use anonymous assessments and a rubric to ensure fairness, focusing on specific, observable aspects of the work.
Lack of specificity	Vague feedback can make students feel their efforts aren't seen or appreciated.	Teach specific feedback stems (e.g., "One thing I liked was..."), focusing on concrete details to show true appreciation.
Fear of hurting feelings	Fear of offending peers can prevent students from giving honest feedback, missing opportunities for mutual support.	Normalize constructive feedback with the Glow and Grow approach, framing feedback as support for one another's success.
Discomfort receiving feedback	Receiving feedback can make students feel vulnerable, affecting their sense of psychological safety and connection.	Discuss the benefits of peer feedback, using self-reflection activities to create a safe, supportive environment.
Overly harsh or critical feedback	Harsh feedback can make students feel judged or excluded, potentially damaging their confidence and belonging.	Teach the Positive Sandwich method to balance feedback with kindness, promoting a respectful and supportive approach.
Inability to identify areas for improvement	Struggling to find constructive feedback can make students feel inadequate or disconnected.	Provide a checklist or rubric, and use group practice to build confidence, making each student feel capable and connected.

(continued)

FIGURE 5.2
Challenge-LENS-Solution (*Continued*)

Challenge	LENS	Solution
Unclear expectations for feedback	Without clear expectations, students may feel uncertain and worry they're "doing it wrong," affecting their sense of belonging.	Use a feedback rubric or checklist and model examples to create clarity and build confidence, fostering a sense of security.
Time constraints	Rushed feedback may make students feel their work isn't valued, reducing opportunities for meaningful connection.	Set aside time for quality feedback on specific areas, reinforcing the idea that students' work and voices are valued in the community.
Fixed mindset toward peer feedback	Students may dismiss peer feedback as being less valuable, missing a chance to connect and learn from one another.	Emphasize the unique value of learning from peers, celebrating feedback as a way to grow together and deepen classroom connection.
Difficulty balancing positive and constructive feedback	Focusing only on positive or only on constructive feedback may feel insincere or critical.	Teach the Two Stars and a Wish method, creating balanced feedback that feels authentic and supportive.
Peer pressure and conformity	Pressure to conform to peers' feedback can reduce authenticity and diversity in perspectives.	Encourage independent thinking, use anonymous forms, and foster an environment where all opinions are valued.
Difficulty translating feedback into action	Struggling to apply feedback can make students feel disconnected from the process.	Teach how to prioritize feedback and set small goals, creating a supportive space where everyone feels capable of growth.

Evaluating the Cultural Impact of Peer Assessments

Once peer assessments have been implemented, it's crucial to reflect on their cultural effectiveness and impact. Consider these guiding questions:

- Did students engage sincerely with the process, showing effort and thoughtfulness in their feedback?
- Did the feedback foster growth and understanding while ensuring students felt supported and respected?
- Were students able to see the value in both their own and their peers' contributions?

Involving students in this reflection process can provide valuable insights. Ask them for feedback on how they felt about the activity, whether they found it helpful, and how it could be improved.

Summing Up and Looking Ahead

Peer assessment, when implemented with cultural sensitivity, transforms the classroom into a community where learning is a shared responsibility and every voice matters. In classrooms with diverse cultural norms—balancing collectivist and individualistic values—peer assessment becomes an opportunity to bridge differences and foster mutual respect.

By adopting culturally aware practices, teachers can guide students to view learning as a collective journey rather than an isolated task. This approach not only enhances academic growth but also builds stronger relationships within the classroom community.

Creating a culturally inclusive, growth-centered classroom involves more than just applying techniques. It requires honoring the values and perspectives students bring with them. Peer assessment, when viewed through this lens, becomes a bridge between classroom goals and cultural realities, empowering students to grow together in meaningful ways.

In the next chapter, we'll explore the pivotal role of empathy in creating a classroom that is both relevant and responsive to students' cultural backgrounds. Empathy is not just a "nice to have" but a *nonnegotiable skill* for teachers—especially when working with students from collectivist cultures who may feel excluded in predominantly individualistic structures. Chapter 6 highlights the power of emotional intelligence and practical strategies to connect with students on a deeper level, paving the way for a more personalized and impactful learning experience.

6

Building Relationships Through Empathy

Allow me to share an experience that changed my perspective on empathy. It was my third year of teaching, and I was feeling confident. I had just relocated from the Virgin Islands to Florida— a new job, a new school, and a fresh start. I was excited. My lesson plans were meticulously crafted, and my classroom rules were posted for all to see. My approach was structured, disciplined, efficient, and—I believed—effective.

But despite my efforts, I noticed something troubling. There was tension among some of my students, particularly those from more communal backgrounds. They seemed disengaged, detached even. Their participation was half-hearted, as if the classroom wasn't theirs. It felt like they were in a space where they didn't truly belong. I couldn't figure out what was missing. I had assumed that a well-organized classroom with clear expectations would naturally engage all my students because that's how I was raised, and it had always worked for me. But my approach was falling short for many of them, especially a quiet girl named Maria.

Maria rarely raised her hand. She spoke softly and often whispered to her friends during group activities or while sitting at her desk. I assumed she was distracted or bored. Honestly, I even called her out a few times, thinking she wasn't paying attention. Any time it came to individual work, I would gently remind her, "Maria, let's get back on task."

Then, one day during a group project, something shifted. I overheard Maria's soft voice offering her classmates detailed explanations on how to approach the task they were working on. She was leading the conversation, guiding them, and encouraging them with confidence. I had never seen this side of her during class discussions. The realization hit me hard: Maria wasn't disengaged; she was simply participating in the way that felt most natural to her. Her behavior wasn't defiance or boredom; it reflected her cultural comfort with collective success over individual recognition.

That evening, I reflected deeply on the day and what I had observed with Maria. My classroom had been designed to value independent work and individual achievement, which matched my upbringing and teaching philosophy—but it didn't resonate with Maria or students like her. I had been so focused on running an orderly, structured classroom that I hadn't stopped to consider whether it was truly inclusive.

That's when I realized empathy wasn't just about listening to students when they spoke. It was about understanding how they felt and why they behaved in certain ways—even when they weren't speaking.

The next day, I made a change. I set aside time to ask my students about their experiences: What made them feel included? What excited them? How did they learn best? Maria's eyes lit up when I asked the class how they felt about group activities versus solo assignments. For the first time, I saw her raise her hand willingly. She shared that she loved group projects because, in her words, they felt like "solving puzzles with friends."

That was the moment I understood that empathy is not a passive trait. It's an active, intentional practice. It's about shifting one's perspective, stepping into the students' world, and teaching in a way that respects and values their experiences.

That realization transformed not only my relationship with my students but the entire atmosphere of my classroom. And it all started with Maria's soft but mighty voice.

Maria taught me that empathy bridges a teacher's intention and a student's connection. Empathy is more than a nice quality; it's a powerful way to build meaningful relationships, especially in a diverse classroom. When teachers show empathy, they create spaces where students feel seen, heard, and valued. Expressing empathy is especially important for students from different cultural backgrounds who may not always feel like they fit in, particularly if they come from cultures that value group connections over individual success.

In this chapter, I'll discuss how empathy helps build stronger relationships in the classroom. By understanding and respecting students' feelings, teachers can create an environment where students feel comfortable being themselves. I'll explore these three areas:

- **Why empathy matters in teaching:** How empathy helps teachers connect with students.
- **Building emotional intelligence:** How teachers can tune into emotions to understand students better.
- **Creating an empathetic classroom:** Strategies for making sure everyone feels included.

Why Empathy Matters in Teaching

A common misconception among teachers about empathy is the belief that connecting with students requires being able to relate to their experiences. In reality, empathy is not about fully understanding someone else's life; it's about finding value and validation in each student's unique background, emotions, and perspectives as they truly are.

The phrase "walk a mile in someone's shoes" is often used to describe empathy, but I struggle with this metaphor. To me, it suggests that understanding someone else is as simple as imagining their experience. Yet, this notion stems from a place of privilege; it implies that one can "walk a mile" and then simply return to their own life.

For the students we serve, their experiences are not a choice; they are lived realities, every single day. They cannot decide when to walk that mile or pause the journey. Empathy requires much more than imagining; it calls for listening, observing, and respecting each student's identity.

Empathy is especially critical in classrooms with students from both individualistic and collectivist cultural backgrounds. These groups often have very different perspectives on success, participation, and collaboration, as noted several times in this book. Here's a reminder of those differences:

- **Individualistic students** value personal achievement, independent work, and self-expression. They often thrive on opportunities to stand out, contribute their ideas independently, and receive personal recognition for their accomplishments.
- **Collectivist students** tend to view success through the lens of group harmony, shared goals, and mutual support.

They may prefer group work, sharing ideas for the benefit of the team, and avoiding actions that could disrupt unity.

In classrooms overly focused on individual achievement, collectivist students may feel overlooked or misunderstood. For example, group-oriented students may see their contributions go unnoticed because they prioritize the success of the team over recognition of themselves.

By practicing empathy, you can bridge these cultural differences, creating a space where both individualistic and collectivist students feel seen, respected, and valued. Doing so involves more than surface-level understanding; it's about recognizing and validating each student's preferred way of learning and participating, ensuring that your classroom supports all cultural norms and every student feels like they belong. Figure 6.1 provides examples of empathy for both individualistic and collectivist students, and the following text describes additional scenarios.

FIGURE 6.1
Examples of Empathy

Grade Level	Empathy for Individualistic Students	Empathy for Collectivist Students
Early childhood	Ms. Jordan notices that Maya loves sharing her artwork during circle time and takes pride in her creations. Ms. Jordan lets Maya take a few moments to show her work to the class individually, affirming her unique contributions and expressing genuine interest in her artistic choices.	Mr. Alvarez sets up a "group story time" during which each child adds to a shared story. He observes that Chen feels more comfortable participating when everyone contributes equally. Mr. Alvarez emphasizes that the story is built through everyone's ideas, making Chen feel proud of the collective outcome without needing individual attention.

(continued)

FIGURE 6.1
Examples of Empathy (*Continued*)

Grade Level	Empathy for Individualistic Students	Empathy for Collectivist Students
Elementary school	Ms. Franklin notices that Olivia excels at science and enjoys standing out through her solo projects. Ms. Franklin encourages Olivia to present her findings to the class and acknowledges her unique insights. She gives Olivia positive feedback on her attention to detail, helping her feel recognized and valued for her individual achievements.	Ms. Kim notices that Ana and her friends prefer to work together on assignments and support each other. Ms. Kim arranges a group activity where they can work as a team on a science project, assigning each member a role that contributes to the group's success. Afterward, she celebrates their shared effort, emphasizing the value of teamwork and cooperation.
Middle school	Mr. Sanchez observes that Liam enjoys contributing his unique ideas during class discussions. He encourages Liam to take a leadership role in a debate, allowing him to showcase his individual insights. Mr. Sanchez provides feedback that highlights Liam's originality and ability to think critically, helping him feel acknowledged for his individual strengths.	Ms. Lopez notices that some of her collectivist students, like Sofia and Carlos, feel most engaged when they work in small groups. She assigns them a collaborative project where they can support each other, then publicly recognizes their teamwork. Ms. Lopez highlights how each student contributed to the group's success, helping Sofia and Carlos feel appreciated as part of a team.
High school	Ms. Thompson realizes that Mark has a strong interest in writing and prefers working independently. She encourages him to pursue an independent study project, allowing him to explore his unique ideas. Ms. Thompson checks in regularly, giving him personalized feedback and support, making him feel recognized for his independent work.	Mr. Lee notices that his collectivist students, like Priya and Ahmed, feel more comfortable working together on assignments. He arranges a group research project on community issues, allowing them to work as a team. Mr. Lee praises their ability to collaborate and find solutions as a group, making Priya and Ahmed feel valued for their collective contributions.

Examples Across All Levels

Empathy belongs in every classroom. Here are some examples to illustrate how it might be evident at various grade levels:

- **Flexible participation options.** In a 5th grade class, Ms. Rivera creates opportunities for her students to choose how they participate in a project showcase. She observes that individualistic students, like Jake, prefer presenting solo, whereas collectivist students, like Mira and Jun, feel more comfortable working together. By offering multiple presentation formats, Ms. Rivera demonstrates empathy and respect for both individualistic and collectivist preferences.
- **Culturally relevant group discussions.** In a high school social studies class, Mr. Patel leads a discussion on cultural identity. Individualistic students, like Sarah, confidently share their opinions, whereas collectivist students, such as Leo and Mei, contribute by building on each other's ideas. Mr. Patel uses his empathetic LENS to create an inclusive environment that values both individual contributions and group collaboration, ensuring all voices are heard.
- **Acknowledging different cultural preferences in feedback.** In a middle school science class, Ms. Dillard assigns group projects but tailors her feedback to suit her students' cultural orientations. For individualistic students, she provides personalized feedback like "Your unique approach added a lot to this project." For collectivist students, she emphasizes teamwork, saying, "I appreciate how well you collaborated and supported each other." This thoughtful approach ensures each student feels valued in ways that resonate with their cultural identity.

Empathy and the Teacher VIBE

Empathy is at the heart of the Teacher VIBE (Valuing Inclusion and Belonging for Everyone) and directly supports creating a classroom where all students feel accepted, supported, and included. By listening, observing, and validating students' unique needs and strengths, you can demonstrate that empathy transforms diversity into an asset rather than a challenge.

You may not always relate to a student's experience, but empathy allows you to listen and show care for their needs. When empathy guides your interactions and decision making, relationships naturally strengthen. As students feel safe, valued, and appreciated, they become more willing to engage, share, and contribute, enhancing the sense of community in your classroom.

Building Your Emotional Intelligence

Emotional intelligence (EI) refers to your ability to understand and manage emotions—both your own and those of others. It plays a crucial role in fostering empathy, facilitating classroom community, and developing meaningful connections with your students. By cultivating EI, you can better recognize and meet the diverse needs of your students in an intentional and culturally responsive way.

At this point, you've likely identified some individualist and collectivist students in your classroom and begun thinking of ways to support their distinct needs. Let's delve deeper into the core components of EI—self-awareness, self-regulation, social awareness, and relationship management—and explore strategies to enhance each one, using your Teacher LENS as a guide.

Self-Awareness

Self-awareness is about tuning into your emotions, triggers, and biases. As discussed in Chapter 1, recognizing your reactions enables you to manage them more effectively and respond thoughtfully. Within the Teacher LENS framework, this corresponds to Looking for biases—acknowledging assumptions that may shape your interactions with students. Here's how to do this:

- **Reflect on your reactions.** After a challenging moment with a student, pause to reflect. Ask yourself the following questions:
  - What emotions did I feel?
  - Were my reactions influenced by personal biases or cultural assumptions? For example, did I misinterpret certain behaviors as negative because they didn't align with my cultural expectations? Identifying these tendencies helps you respond more fairly and empathetically.
- **Keep a reflection journal.** Documenting your experiences allows you to spot recurring patterns in your emotions and behaviors over time. By identifying repeated triggers or biases, you gain opportunities for growth and self-improvement. See Figure 6.2 for sample prompts.
- **Seek feedback.** Invite a trusted colleague to observe your classroom and provide feedback on your interactions with students. They may notice nuances you've overlooked, offering fresh perspectives on your teaching practices. Alternatively, record a lesson and review it later, paying attention to your reactions and interactions. Reflect on how you address student behaviors and whether your responses align with the inclusive classroom you're striving to create.

> **FIGURE 6.2**
> **Prompts for a Reflection Journal**
> 1. What emotions did I feel in response to a challenging situation today?
> 2. What specific triggers made me feel uncomfortable, frustrated, or stressed in class?
> 3. Did I notice any personal assumptions or biases influencing my reaction?
> 4. How might my cultural background or experiences shape my perspective on certain behaviors?
> 5. Did I interpret a student's behavior negatively without considering their perspective?
> 6. In what situations do I feel most in control of my emotions, and why?
> 7. Are there certain behaviors from students that consistently trigger a strong emotional response?
> 8. How do I show empathy when a student is struggling? Could I approach the situation differently?
> 9. What patterns have I noticed in my emotional responses over time?
> 10. When a student challenges me, how do I usually respond? Is there a better approach?
> 11. Are there any cultural or personal biases I hold that might affect how I respond to different students?
> 12. Did I give all students a fair chance to share their perspectives?
> 13. How do I balance expressing authority with empathy in challenging moments?
> 14. How did I handle stress today, and did it affect my teaching or interactions with students?
> 15. What steps can I take to be more patient and understanding in similar situations next time?
> 16. Who could I ask for feedback to gain more insights into my teaching style and interactions?
> 17. How can I actively work on reducing any identified biases or assumptions moving forward?
> 18. What part of my teaching day felt the most rewarding, and what does this say about my values?
> 19. Are there moments when I may have unintentionally dismissed a student's perspective?
> 20. What small steps can I take each day to remain open, empathetic, and self-aware with all students?

Self-Regulation

Self-regulation is the ability to stay calm and composed, even in challenging situations. As educators, we're only human, and it's natural to react emotionally at times. However, by applying your Teacher LENS—particularly by Shifting perspectives and interpreting behavior—you can approach student actions with understanding rather than frustration. Here are some strategies to try:

- **Practice mindful breathing.** When tensions rise, take deep, slow breaths to calm your mind and body. This practice helps you avoid reacting impulsively and gives you space to process the situation thoughtfully.
- **Use a "reset" phrase.** Ground yourself with simple, calming reminders like "Stay calm" or "Be open." These phrases can keep emotions in check, helping you respond constructively rather than emotionally.
- **Pause when needed.** If a conversation becomes heated, it's OK to step back. You might say, "Let's revisit this in a few minutes." This pause allows both you and the student to approach the situation with clarity and composure, showing respect for their perspective.

Social Awareness

Social awareness involves understanding and empathizing with your students' emotions, especially as shaped by their cultural contexts. The Teacher LENS encourages you to Examine verbal and nonverbal communication and Notice group dynamics to better grasp students' feelings and interactions. Here are suggestions for how to do that:

- **Observe nonverbal cues.** Pay close attention to body language, tone of voice, and facial expressions. For example, a slouched posture might signal disengagement, whereas avoiding eye contact could indicate respect in some cultures.
- **Practice active listening.** Show students they're heard by listening attentively, avoiding interruptions, and reflecting on their words. Simple gestures like nodding or paraphrasing their points demonstrate validation.

- **Learn about students' backgrounds.** Familiarize yourself with students' cultural norms, particularly around communication styles. Understanding how they express emotions helps you interpret their behaviors accurately and respond with sensitivity.

Relationship Management

Strong relationships form the foundation of a successful classroom. Through Looking for biases and Noticing group dynamics in the Teacher LENS framework, you can create an environment that values every student's contributions while respecting both individual and group needs. Here are some suggestions for developing strong relationships:

- **Use "I" statements.** Communicate your feelings respectfully with statements like "I feel concerned when. . . ." This approach fosters open dialogue and models healthy emotional expression for your students.
- **Show appreciation regularly.** Celebrate both individual achievements and group successes. For example, you might commend a student's creativity while also acknowledging how a team worked collaboratively to solve a problem.
- **Foster a welcoming atmosphere.** Simple actions like greeting students warmly, using their names, and taking an interest in their lives build a sense of belonging and trust within the classroom.

Combining Emotional Intelligence and the Teacher LENS

Here's how to integrate EI and the Teacher LENS into your teaching practice:

- **Role-play for bias awareness.** Practice addressing challenging scenarios involving students from diverse backgrounds. This activity can reveal implicit biases and help refine your responses.
- **Observe group dynamics regularly.** Pay attention to student roles during group activities. Notice who takes on leadership, who prefers a supporting role, and how cultural norms influence these dynamics.
- **Reframe misunderstandings.** When a student's behavior seems puzzling or challenging, ask yourself, "Could this reflect a cultural norm I don't fully understand?" This question encourages curiosity and respect, reducing the likelihood of misinterpretation.

By blending emotional intelligence with the Teacher LENS, you create a classroom culture that values every student's unique background and an environment where all learners feel seen, respected, and empowered to thrive.

Creating an Empathetic Classroom for Collectivist Students

Creating an empathetic classroom benefits all students, but it's particularly crucial when working with students from collectivist backgrounds. Collectivist students thrive in environments that emphasize connection, collaboration, and shared goals. However, in classrooms that lean heavily toward individualistic practices, their potential can be overlooked. By making intentional choices, you can foster a classroom environment where collectivist students feel valued and experience a strong sense of belonging. Let's examine these choices, including classroom examples and the specific strategies at play.

Focus on Group-Centered Learning

To support collectivist students, prioritize group-centered learning experiences. Activities like project-based learning, gamification, storytelling, and peer assessments (covered in Chapters 4 and 5) give students the opportunity to collaborate and work in ways that resonate with their cultural norms. Teamwork, peer support, and shared goals align with the values of collectivist cultures, helping these students feel comfortable and engaged.

Example in action: Mr. Jackson, a 7th grade science teacher, assigns an ecosystem project that has students working in small groups. Each group selects an ecosystem and assigns specific roles—Researcher, Presenter, Illustrator, and so on—based on individual strengths. Mr. Jackson emphasizes that each role is vital and the group's success depends on everyone's contributions. By prioritizing teamwork over individual recognition, Mr. Jackson ensures his collectivist students feel valued as part of a collective effort.

Strategy: Design collaborative activities with clear roles and responsibilities. When collectivist students see their contributions as essential to group success, they are more likely to feel engaged and connected.

Recognize and Celebrate Group Success

Although individual achievements often take center stage in schools, collectivist students are more motivated by shared accomplishments. Celebrating group successes acknowledges the importance of teamwork and makes collectivist students feel appreciated without singling out individuals.

Example in action: Ms. Chen, a 5th grade teacher, assigns groups to do presentations on historical events. After the presentations, she praises each team for their cooperation and teamwork, saying, "Your group did an amazing job working together!" To further celebrate their efforts, she hands out team certificates that highlight their collective achievements. This recognition ensures her collectivist students feel seen and appreciated without the discomfort of individual attention.

Strategy: Celebrate team achievements with certificates, group celebrations, or classroom shout-outs. This approach reinforces a sense of unity and recognizes the collective effort of all team members.

Set Up the Classroom for Group Belonging

As discussed in Chapter 2, the physical setup of your classroom reflects your Teacher VIBE and influences how students feel about their learning environment. For collectivist students, seating arrangements that promote interaction and connection—like clusters or circles—can foster a sense of community. Avoid isolating students in rows, as this can make collectivist students feel disconnected.

Example in action: Ms. Thomas, a 4th grade teacher, arranges her students' desks into clusters of four or five. This setup encourages group collaboration during projects and casual interaction during discussions. Even during independent work, the arrangement allows students to quietly share ideas or ask questions. For collectivist students, this seating plan creates a sense of connection and comfort.

Strategy: Use flexible seating arrangements like clusters or circles to encourage interaction. This layout helps collectivist students feel part of a community and facilitates natural collaboration.

Build Classroom Community Agreements Together

Involving students in creating classroom community agreements, as discussed in Chapter 2, fosters a sense of shared responsibility and collective ownership, aligning well with collectivist values. When students contribute their ideas to shape the classroom environment, it reinforces the concept of shared space and mutual respect.

Example in action: At the beginning of the school year, Mr. Patel, a 9th grade teacher, involves his students in creating their classroom community agreement. He divides the class into small groups and asks each group to brainstorm what they need to feel accepted and included. After sharing and voting on the final list of agreements, Mr. Patel emphasizes that these agreements reflect shared values and are a collective responsibility. His collectivist students appreciate the collaborative approach, which mirrors their cultural emphasis on group harmony.

Strategy: Collaborate on classroom agreements to emphasize respect, cooperation, and shared values. This process helps collectivist students feel that their contributions are valued and fosters a strong sense of belonging.

Use Empathy in Conflict Resolution

Conflicts are inevitable in any classroom. Addressing them empathetically can promote understanding and collective harmony. Instead of relying on traditional disciplinary measures that isolate or remove students, restorative practices (discussed in Chapter 2) can be used to repair relationships and foster a sense of collective responsibility. These practices align with collectivist students' preferences for resolving conflicts in ways that prioritize group harmony over individual punishment.

Example in action: When a conflict arises between students in her 6th grade classroom, Ms. Green doesn't focus solely on the individuals involved. Instead, she considers how the issue affects the entire classroom and initiates a restorative circle. All students, including those not directly involved, are invited to share their feelings and offer support. This process shows the class that the community is there to help repair relationships and strengthen bonds, rather than simply punishing behavior. Collectivist students feel reassured by this approach, which aligns with their values of empathy, group harmony, and mutual respect.

Strategy: Implement restorative practices such as circles or group discussions to resolve conflicts. This approach emphasizes empathy, understanding, and collective growth, helping collectivist students feel supported.

Build Peer Support Networks

Peer support systems such as project-based learning (discussed in Chapter 4) and peer assessments (discussed in Chapter 5) are powerful tools for fostering collaboration and belonging among collectivist students. Pairing or grouping students for assignments or projects provides them with opportunities to connect, support one another, and thrive in a learning environment that values community.

Example in action: In his high school language arts class, Mr. Lucas assigns "peer learning partners" for weekly assignments. Students are encouraged to discuss readings and help each other with challenging passages. Mr. Lucas notices that collectivist students like Shreya and David are more comfortable engaging in this format than speaking in front of the entire class. This peer support system allows them to participate meaningfully without feeling the pressure of individual attention.

Strategy: Set up peer-learning partnerships or small groups to provide collectivist students with opportunities to connect and learn collaboratively in ways that align with their cultural preferences.

Bring Cultural Stories and Group Discussions into Lessons

Incorporating cultural narratives and group-based discussions into your lessons ensures that collectivist students feel seen and heard. Storytelling (discussed in Chapter 4) and other activities that invite students to share cultural perspectives foster inclusivity and show students that their backgrounds are valued.

Example in action: Ms. Tan, a 6th grade social studies teacher, integrates stories and perspectives from various cultures into her lessons on community and leadership. She facilitates collaborative discussions where students explore how these themes connect to their personal or cultural experiences. This approach helps collectivist students feel represented in the curriculum and more comfortable participating in discussions.

Strategy: Use cultural narratives and group discussions to connect students' backgrounds with lesson content. This approach validates collectivist students' experiences and strengthens their engagement.

Summing Up and Looking Ahead

Empathy and emotional intelligence are essential tools for building authentic relationships with students. Empathy goes beyond simply understanding a student's experiences; it involves creating a classroom environment where every student feels valued and supported.

This chapter highlighted how empathetic strategies can make a meaningful difference, particularly for collectivist students who might struggle in a system that prioritizes individual achievement. By embracing collaborative activities, celebrating group successes, and incorporating culturally responsive practices, you create a classroom where collectivist students can thrive.

Empathy also fosters deeper connections with students by recognizing their unique needs and strengths. When students feel understood and respected, they are more likely to engage, share, and contribute to the classroom community.

Looking ahead to the final chapter, A Call for Adaptive Teaching, we reflect on how empathy serves as the foundation for long-lasting change. The chapter will provide strategies for applying the concepts discussed throughout this book, empowering you to create a classroom—and a school—where every student feels like they belong.

7

A Call for Adaptive Teaching

As we reach the end of this journey, I want to leave you with a simple yet powerful challenge: Let's make our classrooms—and ultimately our schools—places where all students feel valued, supported, and included.

Culturally sensitive teaching practices are not just concepts for occasional application; they are commitments to creating transformative spaces in education. Adaptive teaching requires us to embrace learning, question old habits, and focus on inclusion, ensuring that every student's unique background is acknowledged and valued.

Let's revisit some of the key strategies discussed throughout this book and explore how you can bring them into your teaching practices. Together, we can create classrooms that reflect the diverse cultural identities of our students and promote their academic and personal success.

Find Balance in Your Classroom

From the outset, we discussed how Western education systems often emphasize individualism, with a focus on personal achievements, independence, and competition. For students from collectivist backgrounds, who value group harmony and shared goals, this focus can create challenges and feelings of exclusion. For this reason, it's important to balance individualism and collectivism in the classroom, following suggestions such as these:

- Create activities that integrate both individual and group elements. For example, a class project can include personal reflection assignments alongside group collaboration.
- Celebrate individual achievements while also recognizing and rewarding group successes.
- Design your classroom as a blend of these approaches, ensuring every student feels recognized without needing to assimilate into norms that may not align with their cultural values.

By intentionally embracing both perspectives, you foster an inclusive environment where students don't have to leave parts of their identity behind to succeed.

Bring Cultural Awareness into Everyday Teaching

Cultural awareness goes beyond knowledge; it's about action. It's not just a matter of recognizing the diversity in your classroom but embedding that awareness into your daily teaching practices. Here are some steps to follow to foster everyday cultural awareness:

- **Reflect on your own cultural awareness.** Use tools like the Self-Assessment for Cultural Awareness (Figure 1.2 in Chapter 1) to identify areas for growth.
- **Design inclusive learning experiences.** Alternate between group projects and independent assignments. Use literature, historical events, or case studies that reflect your students' backgrounds.
- **Create a flexible environment.** Whether it's flexible seating arrangements or providing options for how students participate, make your classroom a place where students with diverse preferences feel at home.

Like the refrigerator analogy described in Chapter 1, your classroom setup reflects your values. Thoughtful changes can ensure that all students feel like they belong and have what they need to succeed.

Rethink Classroom Management as Classroom *Community*

Traditional classroom management often focuses on compliance, which may stifle student expression, particularly for those from collectivist cultures. Instead of focusing on control, shift toward building a classroom community that emphasizes inclusion and shared responsibility. Here are some suggestions for how to do that:

- **Adopt the Teacher VIBE mindset.** Valuing Inclusion and Belonging for Everyone means engaging students in shaping their environment. Involve them in crafting classroom

agreements and protocols (as discussed in Chapter 2) and use restorative practices to resolve conflicts.
- **Use flexible seating and participation options.** Structuring your classroom to allow for collaboration and individual work ensures that students can thrive in their preferred settings.
- **Celebrate diverse achievements.** Recognize students in ways that align with their values, whether through individual recognition or group success.

This shift not only fosters belonging but also encourages engagement and builds trust between students and teachers.

Sharpen Your Observational Skills with the Teacher LENS

Throughout my years as an educator, I've learned that a critical aspect of adaptive teaching is understanding that behavior often carries a cultural context. However, as human beings, these behaviors may be misinterpreted based on our biases. What might appear as disengagement or distraction could actually be an expression of a student's cultural norms and values. By sharpening your observational skills through the Teacher LENS framework, you can better interpret these behaviors and respond in ways that feel supportive rather than punitive.

The Teacher LENS encourages you to take a moment to look deeper into the behavior you are observing. It also requires you to recognize that each student brings a unique way of engaging based on their cultural background. By applying this framework, you're better equipped to nurture an inclusive classroom atmosphere where all students are encouraged to express themselves authentically. Ultimately, observation through this

LENS helps you understand and appreciate your students on a deeper level, building connections based on respect and mutual understanding.

Foster Collaboration with Project-Based Learning and Storytelling

Building a collective, inclusive classroom environment means embedding instructional practices that emphasize teamwork and community. Project-based learning, storytelling, and even gamification offer effective ways to foster a sense of collaboration among students, allowing them to connect with each other and engage with the material in a way that feels meaningful.

In a PBL framework, students work together to solve real-world problems, drawing on their unique strengths and experiences. This approach invites students to see how collaboration enriches their learning, as they bring their perspectives together to achieve common goals. Storytelling, similarly, gives students from various backgrounds the chance to share their narratives, helping to build empathy and mutual understanding among classmates. When we listen to each other's stories, we see beyond the surface, recognizing the value each student contributes to the overall classroom community.

Adopt Peer Assessments to Build Community

Peer assessments can be a great tool to build community. When done with cultural sensitivity, students support each other in their growth. Considering your classroom with a mixture of collectivist and individualist students, peer assessments provide a space for collaborative growth, allowing students to offer constructive feedback in a way that respects and values each person's effort.

As you teach students ways to give feedback to their peers, consider highlighting the importance of giving and receiving feedback not only as a learning opportunity but as a community-building exercise. Encourage your students to offer positive, constructive feedback, focusing on both achievements and areas for growth. This approach allows them to feel invested in each other's success, helping them develop empathy and a sense of shared accomplishment.

Reflect on Empathy as the Foundation of Your VIBE

At the core of your VIBE is empathy. Throughout this book, I've emphasized empathy as a starting point for creating a culturally responsive classroom. Practicing empathy allows you to see the world from your students' point of view, understanding their unique experiences and needs. It's not about making assumptions based on their zip code, last names, or what other limited information you may know about your students. It's about forming a lasting bond and recognizing the beauty in diversity and the value each student brings to the learning environment.

As you continue your journey as an educator, remember that empathy is more than a tool; it's a way of being that can alter your instructional practices and ultimately your students' experiences. Approach each interaction with understanding and compassion to create a classroom that is not only a place for academics but a community where each student feels accepted, supported, and included.

A Final Call to Action

As you consider the strategies outlined in this book, remember that whatever adaptations you make in your teaching will take time to put into practice. Start small by implementing one or two ideas as you develop your VIBE. Perhaps during this marking period, you could focus on your seating arrangements and on developing a classroom community agreement. Follow that up by using the Teacher LENS to observe student behavior or involving students in peer assessments. Over time, these practices will become second nature, and you'll see the positive impact on your students and your classroom culture. Adaptive teaching is an ongoing journey, and your commitment to it is a powerful force for positive change.

Learn from your students, challenge your biases, and approach your teaching with curiosity and cultural sensitivity. By doing so, you'll cultivate classrooms that celebrate and support individualist and collectivist student success. Together, we can build schools that are not just places of education but communities of belonging. The future of teaching is adaptive. Let's embrace it.

Acknowledgments

Every time I have the opportunity to write a book about something I'm passionate about, I consider it a true blessing. But I could never do this work sharing my experiences, research, and insight without the support and inspiration of others.

First and foremost, I want to acknowledge my two kids, Laila and SJ. Thank you for your patience during this process, the subtle motivation, the jokes, the jabs, and the roast sessions that pushed me to be the best version of myself—a version that makes you proud to call me your dad.

To my siblings, Colleen and Justin, thank you for always being in my corner. Your encouragement and advice mean more than you know.

I'm also deeply grateful to my parents, Lewis and Denese, for modeling what it means to follow your dreams and leave a legacy that matters.

To my professional colleagues and the incredible guests on the *Leading Equity* podcast, your conversations, insights, and dedication to education have been a constant source of inspiration for this book. Thank you for showing up, leading with heart, and pushing the work forward.

To the team at ASCD, especially Bill Varner and Liz Wegner, thank you for your guidance and support throughout this project. Your partnership has meant a great deal.

And finally, to the educators working tirelessly each day to make students feel seen, safe, and valued, you are the reason for this book. The work is hard, but your impact is profound. Keep going. You're changing lives and shaping futures.

References

Ahmad, A., & Law, E. L.-C. (2021). Educators as gamemasters: Creating serious role playing game with "ARQS." *Proceedings of the ACM on Human-Computer Interaction, 5*(CHI PLAY), 1–29.

Almulla, M. A. (2020, July–September). The effectiveness of the project-based learning (PBL) approach as a way to engage students in learning. *Sage Open, 10*(3).

Atiku, N. A. (2021). Storytelling and the preservation of Indigenous culture in Nigeria. *Chukwuemeka Odumegwu Ojukwu Journal of Folklore and Cultural Studies, 1*(1).

Berrebbah, I. (2020). The politics and aesthetics of storytelling in Diana Abu-Jaber's *Crescent*: A strategic implementation of an old folkloric Arab tradition. *English Studies at NBU, 6*(1), 127–144.

Bluteau, J., Aubenas, S., & Dufour, F. (2022). Influence of flexible classroom seating on the wellbeing and mental health of upper elementary school students: A gender analysis. *Frontiers in Psychology, 13*.

Cheryan, S., Ziegler, S. A., Plaut, V. C., & Meltzoff, A. N. (2014). Designing classrooms to maximize student achievement. *Policy Insights from the Behavioral and Brain Sciences, 1*(1), 4–12.

Christopoulos, A., & Mystakidis, S. (2023). Gamification in education. *Encyclopedia, 3*(4), 1223–1243.

Craddock, D. L. (2021). *Dungeon hacks: How NetHack, Angband, and other roguelikes changed the course of video games.* CRC Press.

Darling-Hammond, S. (2023). *Fostering belonging, transforming schools: The impact of restorative practices.* Learning Policy Institute. https://learningpolicyinstitute.org/product/impact-restorative-practices-brief

Darling-Hammond, S., & Fronius, T. (2023). Restorative practices in schools. In E. J. Sabornie & D. L. Espelage (Eds.), *Handbook of classroom management* (3rd ed., pp. 54–73). Routledge.

Eakins, S. L. (2022). *Leading equity: Becoming an advocate for all students.* Jossey-Bass.

Eakins, S. L. (Host). (2024a, April 8). LE 341: How storytelling bridges generations and cultures in education, with Nawal Qarooni [Audio podcast episode]. *Leading Equity.* https://www.leadingequitycenter.com/341

Eakins, S. L. (Host). (2024b, October 7). LE 355: Project-based learning myths: What you need to know [Audio podcast episode]. *Leading Equity.* https://www.leadingequitycenter.com/355

Eerkes-Medrano, L., & Huntington, H. P. (2021). Untold stories: Indigenous knowledge beyond the changing Arctic cryosphere. *Frontiers in Climate, 3.*

German, J. D., Villapando, K. D. C., Resilva, J. P., Quiambao, J. R. C., & Guevarra, A. R. (2020, April). Effects of various seating arrangements on academic performance of grade 11 students in statistics. In *2020 IEEE 7th International Conference on Industrial Engineering and Applications (ICIEA)*, 953–957.

Gremmen, M. C., van den Berg, Y. H. M., Segers, E., & Cillessen, A. H. N. (2016). Considerations for classroom seating arrangements and the role of teacher characteristics and beliefs. *Social Psychology of Education, 19*(4), 749–774.

Grethlein, J. (2023). *Ancient Greek texts and modern narrative theory.* Cambridge University Press.

Gülmez, D., & Ordu, A. (2022). Back to the classroom: Teachers' views on classroom management after Covid-19. *International Journal of Modern Education Studies, 6*(2), 257–286.

Haensel, J. X., Smith, T. J., & Senju, A. (2021). Cultural differences in mutual gaze during face-to-face interactions: A dual head-mounted eye-tracking study. *Visual Cognition, 30*(1–2), 100–115.

Haiken, M. (2017). *Gamify literacy: Boost comprehension, collaboration, and learning.* International Society for Technology in Education.

Hammond, Z. L. (2015). *Culturally responsive teaching and the brain: Promoting authentic engagement and rigor among culturally and linguistically diverse students.* Corwin.

Hofstede, G. H. (2001). *Culture's consequences: Comparing values, behaviors, institutions, and organizations across nations* (2nd ed.). Sage.

Hofstede, G., Hofstede, G. J., & Minkov, M. (2010). *Cultures and organizations: Software of the mind* (3rd ed.). McGraw-Hill.

Jackson, S. C., Chubb, L. A., Paris, S., & de Haan, I. (2024). Te Wāhi Whangai methodology: A nurturing space for storytelling, achievement, and research. *Qualitative Social Work, 24*(2–3), 242–263.

Kirschner, P. A. (2017). Stop propagating the learning styles myth. *Computers & Education, 106,* 166–171.

Kohn, A. (2021, September 17). The classroom-management field can't stop chasing the wrong goal. *Education Week*. https://www.edweek.org/teaching-learning/opinion-the-classroom-management-field-cant-stop-chasing-the-wrong-goal/2021/09

Lilomaiava-Doktor, S. I. (2020). Oral traditions, cultural significance of storytelling, and Samoan understandings of place or fanua. *Native American and Indigenous Studies, 7*(1), 121–151.

Lodi, E., Perrella, L., Lepri, G. L., Scarpa, M. L., & Patrizi, P. (2021). Use of restorative justice and restorative practices at school: A systematic literature review. *International Journal of Environmental Research and Public Health, 19*(1), 96.

Nehyba, J., Juhanák, L., & Cigán, J. (2021). Effects of seating arrangement on students' interaction in group reflective practice. *The Journal of Experimental Education, 91*(2), 249–277.

Peterson, J. (2020). *The elusive shift: How role-playing games forged their identity*. MIT Press.

Poku, V. (2022). *Black student teachers' experiences of racism in the white school: Strategies of resilience and survival*. Palgrave Macmillan.

Price, M., & Pace, D. (2005). Instructional techniques to facilitate inclusive education. In D. Schwartz (Ed.), *Including children with special needs: A handbook for educators and parents* (pp. 115–131). Greenwood Press.

Qarooni, N. (2024). *Nourishing caregiver collaborations: Elevating home experiences and classroom practices for collective care*. Routledge.

Ranco, D., & Haverkamp, J. (2022). Storying Indigenous (life) worlds: An introduction. *Genealogy, 6*(2), 25.

Reilly, M. (2023). Maui, Polynesian culture hero: A nineteenth century tradition from Ruapuke Island. *Journal of New Zealand Studies*, (35), 7–21.

Sackstein, S. (2024). *Student-led assessment: Promoting agency and achievement through portfolios and conferences*. ASCD.

Salma, C., & Şahin, A. (2022). Evaluation of the seating arrangements in English language classrooms through multiple perspectives. *European Journal of Education Studies, 9*(11).

Shin, L. J., Armenta, C. N., Kamble, S. V., Chang, S. L., Wu, H. Y., & Lyubomirsky, S. (2020). Gratitude in collectivist and individualist cultures. *The Journal of Positive Psychology, 15*(5), 598–604.

Syaifullah, A., Munir, M., & Ariyani. A. (2022). An analysis of seating arrangement on students' learning attention. *Journal of Excellence in English Language Education, 1*(1).

Tobia, V., Sacchi, S., Cerina, V., Manca, S., & Fornara, F. (2022). The influence of classroom seating arrangement on children's cognitive processes in primary school: The role of individual variables. *Current Psychology, 41*(9), 6522–6533.

Tomlinson, C. A. (2023, March 6). What no one told me about "classroom management" as a new teacher [Blog post]. *ASCD Blog*. https://www.ascd.org/blogs/what-no-one-told-me-about-classroom-management-as-a-new-teacher

Wolff, C. E., Jarodzka, H., & Boshuizen, H. P. A. (2021). Classroom management scripts: A theoretical model contrasting expert and novice teachers' knowledge and awareness of classroom events. *Educational Psychology Review, 33*(1), 131–148.

Yang, X., Zhou, X., & Hu, J. (2021). Students' preferences for seating arrangements and their engagement in cooperative learning activities in college English blended learning classrooms in higher education. *Higher Education Research & Development, 41*(4), 1356–1371.

Zakszeski, B., & Rutherford, L. (2021). Mind the gap: A systematic review of research on restorative practices in schools. *School Psychology Review, 50*(2-3), 371–387.

Zamani, A. (2022). A structural study of narrative in Irish myths and folktales. *Advances in Language and Literary Studies, 13*(2), 68–80.

Zhang, S., & Pell, M. D. (2022). Cultural differences in vocal expression analysis: Effects of task, language, and stimulus-related factors. *PLoS ONE, 17*(10).

Index

The letter *f* following a page locator denotes a figure.

accomplishment, celebrating, 50
accountability, PBL in building, 102
achievement, celebrating and respecting, 49
activities
    balancing for cultural awareness, 32
    balancing the VIBE, 50
    feedback, 148–153
    gamification, 124–127
    individualistic vs. collectivist, 35
    peer assessment, 139–141
    project-based learning, 98–99, 99*f*, 100–101
    storytelling, 111–113
    verbal processing in group, 84–85
appreciation, showing, 174
Art Critique Circle (activity), 139–140
assessment. *See* peer assessment
assignments
    culturally sensitive, 40
    individualistic vs. collectivist, 33–37
avatars, 118, 119–120*f*, 120–122, 122*f*, 123

badge and achievement systems, 132*f*
balance, finding in the classroom, 183
behavior
    biases when interpreting, 74–75
    classroom community agreements for, 59–61
    cultural norms in, 78
    individualistic vs. collectivist, 35, 37–38, 78, 80–81
    using the LENS to reduce misinterpretations of, 76–81, 86, 89–92

behavioral issues
    alternative approaches to, 22–25
    talking out of turn, 79–80
    vignette, 21–22
belonging
    classroom set-up for group, 177–178
    creating a sense of, 31, 97–98
    feedback and, 143, 144
    gamification and, 118
biases
    LENS framework in looking for, 74–75, 79, 81, 88–91
    understanding, 31
Bingo (activity), 98–99, 99*f*
breathing, mindful, 173

celebrations, 49–50
circles, restorative, 57
classroom community agreements, 58–61, 178
Classroom Community Agreement sample, 62*f*
classroom management
    behavioral issues. *see* behavioral issues
    building a student-centered community agreement, 58–61, 62*f*
    flexible expectations in, 92
    Red Light, Green Light approach, 70–72
    responsive, 33
    restorative practices, 56–58
    seating arrangements, 43, 63–67, 63*f*
    Self-Assessment for Classroom Environment, 51, 52–55*f*

classroom management (cont'd)
    Teacher VIBE in promoting harmony, 50
    traditional, 42–45, 67
classrooms. *See also* gamification
    as community, 138, 184–185
    connecting through PBL, 96–104
    cultural awareness, integrating, 25–26
    economy or reward system, 132*f*
    empathetic for collectivists, 175–180
    finding balance in, 183
    individualistic vs. collectivist, 18–20, 37–38
    setting up for group belonging, 177–178
    welcoming, building, 174
The Class Story Tree (activity), 112–113
collaboration
    advocating for, the VIBE and, 50
    fostering, 186
    intentionally teaching skills of, 40
collaborative science experiments, 105*f*
collaborative seating zones, 63*f*, 65
collectivist classrooms, 95, 175–180
collectivist cultures. *See also* individualistic vs. collectivist cultures
    behavioral issues and, 21–25
    impact of individualism on, 11–13
communication
    building skills with peer assessment, 138
    in collectivist settings, 84
    conversations, restorative, 57–58
    culturally aware, 32
    indirect vs. direct, 88*f*, 90–91
    tone of voice in, 88*f*, 89–90
    verbal and nonverbal, 75, 79, 81, 85, 88–92
communication styles through the LENS framework
    direct eye contact vs. avoidance, 87–89, 88*f*
    indirect vs. direct communication, 88*f*, 90–91
    tone of voice, 88*f*, 89–90
community
    building with peer assessment, 186–187
    classrooms as, 58–61, 62*f*, 184–185
community service projects, 105*f*
confidence, peer assessment to build, 139
conflict resolution, empathy in, 178–179
conform, pressure to, 12–13
conversations, restorative, 57–58

critical-thinking skills, peer assessment to build, 138
cross-cultural understanding, Teacher VIBE in promoting, 49
cultural awareness
    developing, 31–33
    feedback stems to encourage, 143–144, 145–146*f*, 147–148
    fostering in everyday teaching, 183–184
    integrating, 25–26
    PBL in fostering, 103
    reflecting on and developing, 27–28
    self-assessment for, 28, 29–30*f*
    Teacher VIBE in promoting, 49
cultural dimensions model (Hofstede), 26–27
cultural exchange projects, 106*f*
cultural heritage exhibitions, 105*f*
cultural responsiveness, PBL in fostering, 103
culture
    defining, 5–6
    in education, 4–5
    individualistic, 8–13
    learning styles vs., 3–4
    Red Light, Green Light example, 70–72
cultures. *See also* collectivist cultures; individualistic vs. collectivist cultures
    breaking barriers between, 110–111
    storytelling as a bridge between, 114, 117
    Teacher LENS, developing a, 6–7
    that revere storytelling, 109*f*

debate
    historical, 106*f*
    story-based, 116*f*
desk areas, independent, 63*f*, 64–65
desks, dual-purpose, 63*f*, 64
digital storytelling, 116*f*
discipline, alternatives to, 24–25
documentary film project, 105*f*

education
    culture in, 4–5, 13
    individualism and, 9–11
    individualistic vs. collectivist approaches, 18–20
Elevator Pitch (activity), 35
emotional intelligence (EI), 170–175
empathy
    connecting with, 32–33
    examples of, 167–168*f*, 169

Index 197

feedback and, 147
function of, 164–165
peer assessment to build, 139
Teacher VIBE and, 170, 187
in teaching, importance of, 166–167
engagement, 49, 83
entertainment, individualism in, 9
entrepreneurial projects, 106*f*
environmental action plan, 106*f*
escape room-style learning, 131*f*
expectations
    classroom community agreements for, 59–61
    flexible, 92
eye contact vs. avoidance, 87–89, 88*f*

failure, redefining, 128
families, engaging with storytelling, 110–111
feedback
    activities, 148–153
    building EI, 171
    culturally responsive, 143–144
    positive and constructive, 145–146*f*
    specific and observable, 147
    teaching, 141–143
Feedback Bingo (activity), 150
Feedback Fishbowl (activity), 152–153
Feedback Journal Exchange (activity), 151–152
Feedback Ladder (activity), 151
feedback stems, 143–144, 145–146*f*, 147–148
Five Things You Should Know About Me (activity), 111

Gallery Walk with Feedback Sticky Notes (activity), 149
gamification
    about, 117
    activities, 124–127
    avatars, 118, 119–120*f*, 120–122, 122*f*, 123
    belonging and, 118
    for collectivists and individualists, 130, 131–132*f*
    getting started with, 129–130
    for individualist and collectivist cultures, 128
    power of, 130
    redefining failure, 128
garden project, school or classroom, 105*f*
Getting to Know You (activity), 100–101
global pen pals, 106*f*
Glow and Grow Circles (activity), 152

Glow and Grow feedback, 142, 147
GPA tracking, individualism in, 9
grading, peer assessment vs. peer, 136–137
group discussion
    incorporating into lessons, 180
    Teacher LENS framework, scenarios, 86
group dynamics, LENS framework in noticing, 75–76, 80–81, 85, 89, 92
group work
    a discipline alternative, 24
    group-centered learning, 176
    story creation, 115*f*
    verbal processing in, 84–85
growth mindset, 144

historical reenactment, 106*f*
historical storytelling, 115*f*
Hofstede, Geert, 26–27
horn effect, 21–22

inclusion, feedback stems to encourage, 144
individualism, 8–13
individualistic vs. collectivist cultures
    behavior, impact on, 35, 37–38, 78
    cultural dimensions model (Hofstede), 26–27, 27*f*
    engagement in, 83
    gamification and, 128
    in project-based learning, 101–102
    Red Light, Green Light example, 70–72
    storytelling in, 107–108
individualists vs. collectivists
    activities for, 35
    assignments for, 33–37
    behavior, 80–81
    belonging, 47–48
    building bonds with, 48
    characteristics of, 166–167
    classrooms for, 18–20, 37–38
    inclusion, 46–47
    peer assessment, 137–138
    seating arrangements, 43
    valuing, 46
    vignette, 163–165
inspiration, 138
instruction
    assignments, individualistic vs. collectivist, 33–37
    tailoring for cultural awareness, 31–33
interactive learning platforms, 132*f*
"I" statements, 174

judgments, making fair, 33

leaderboards with team goals, 131*f*
learning
  deeper, Teacher VIBE in promoting, 50
  peer assessment and, 138
learning corners, personalized, 63*f*, 66
learning styles, culture vs., 3–4
Legend of Zelda (Nintendo), 94
listening, active, 173

movement breaks, a discipline alternative, 24–25
myth and legend creation, 115*f*

nonverbal cues in social awareness, 173

observation practices
  building bridges through, 81
  Teacher LENS, 73, 77, 185–186

parent-teacher conferences, individualism in, 9
peer assessment
  activities, 139–141
  aligned with Teacher VIBE, 141
  benefits of, 136–139, 141
  to build community, 186–187
  challenges and solutions, 158, 159–160*f*
  cultural impact, evaluating the, 161
  done correctly (examples), 153–158
  feedback in, 141–143
  peer grading vs., 136–137
  strategies, 148–153
Peer Feedback Carousel (activity), 149–150
Peer Feedback Role-Playing (activity), 150–151
peers helping peers, 80–81, 85–86
peer story exchange, 116*f*
peer support networks, 179–180
perimeter clusters, 63*f*, 64
play, power of, 130
Positive Sandwich feedback, 142
problem-solving
  collective, LENS framework scenarios, 85–86
  narrative based, 116*f*
project-based learning (PBL)
  about, 96–98
  accountability, building, 102
  activities, 98–99, 99*f*, 100–101
  for collectivists, modifications for individualists, 105–106*f*

cultural responsiveness, fostering, 103
fostering collaboration with, 186
individualistic vs. collectivist cultures in, 101–102
planning for successful, 103–104

quest games, 131*f*

Red Light, Green Light, 70–72
reflection journals, building EI, 171, 172*f*
Reflection on a Science Experiment (activity), 140–141
refrigerators as cultural reflections, 17–20
relationship management, 174
report cards, individualism in, 9
reset phrases, 173
respect
  feedback stems to encourage, 144
  peer assessment to build, 138
responsibility
  collective, Teacher VIBE and, 49
  peer assessment to strengthen, 138
restorative practices, 56–58
reward systems, 132*f*
role-playing games, 132*f*
rotational seating, 63*f*, 65

seating arrangements, 43, 63–67, 63*f*
Self-Assessment for Classroom Environment, 52–55*f*
Self-Assessment for Cultural Awareness, 29–30*f*
self-awareness, building EI, 171
self-expression, creating spaces for, 50
self-help culture, individualism and, 8
self-reflection
  on cultural awareness, 27–28
  for culturally responsive teaching, 40
  feedback for, 147
  journaling for, 171, 172*f*
  peer assessment and, 138
self-regulation, building EI, 172–173
Sentence-Starter Cards (activity), 152
silence in collectivist cultures, 12
simulation games, 132*f*
social awareness, building EI, 173–174
social expectations, individualism and, 8
sports, individualism in, 9
standardized testing, individualism in, 9
storytelling
  activities, 111–113
  benefits of, 104, 107
  challenges in a diverse classroom, 113–114

for collectivists, modifications for individualists, 114, 115–116*f*
cultures that revere, 109*f*
for family engagement, 110–111
fostering collaboration with, 186
incorporate cultural narratives, 180
for individualistic and collectivist students, 107–108
storytelling circles, 115*f*
strengths, finding, 2–3
students
bonding with, 32–33, 48
buy-in, Teacher VIBE and, 49
embarrassing, 136
learning about, 174
student-teacher relationships, classroom management and, 44
success
individualism in measuring, 10–11
recognize and celebrate, 49–50, 176–177

Teacher LENS
developing a, 6–7
observation practices, 73
strategies for using, 91–92
Teacher LENS framework
combining EI with the, 174–175
observing with purpose, 77
peer assessment challenges and solutions, 158, 159–160*f*
to reduce misinterpretations of behavior, 77–81
Teacher LENS framework, communication styles through the
direct eye contact vs. avoidance, 87–89, 88*f*
indirect vs. direct communication, 88*f*, 90–91
tone of voice, 88*f*, 89–90
Teacher LENS framework, scenarios
collective problem solving, 85–86
group discussion, 86
helping peers, 85–86
verbal engagement, 86
verbal processing in group activities, 84–85

Teacher LENS framework components
examine verbal and nonverbal communication, 75, 79, 81, 85, 88–92
look for biases, 74–75, 79, 81, 88–91
notice group dynamics, 75–76, 80–81, 85, 89, 92
shift perspectives and interpret behavior, 76–81, 86, 89–92
teachers, individualistic, in collectivist environments, 82–84
Teacher VIBE (Valuing Inclusion and Belonging for Everyone)
belonging component, 47–48
benefits, 49–50
classroom self-assessment, 51, 52–55*f*
empathy and, 170
empathy in the, 187
everyone component, 48
importance of, 48–49
inclusion component, 46–47
purpose, 46
restorative practices, 56–58
strategies for balancing the, 50
valuing component, 46
teaching
importance of empathy in, 166–167
strategies for culturally responsive, 39–40
team-based challenges and competitions, 131*f*
tone of voice, 88*f*, 89–90
troublemaker label, 21
trust, building, 137
Two Stars and a Wish (activity), 149

U-shaped seating, 63*f*, 66

verbal engagement, 86
verbal processing in group activities, 84–85

What's Your Classroom Avatar? (activity), 124–127
Writing Assignment Peer Review (activity), 140

About the Author

Sheldon L. Eakins, PhD, is an experienced school administrator, education consultant, author, speaker, and founder of Purposeful Teaching Academy. His mission is to help educators create student-centered learning environments where all students thrive. Eakins specializes in leadership development, school culture, and practical strategies that support teaching with clarity and purpose.

He holds a BS in social science education, an MS in educational leadership, and a PhD in K–12 studies. He brings more than 15 years of experience across K–12 and higher education, including roles in special education, alternative education, and school administration.

Through the Purposeful Teaching Academy, Eakins partners with schools to deliver personalized keynotes, workshops, and coaching that foster strong relationships, boost engagement, and support lasting change in teaching and leadership practices.

To learn more about Eakins's work, visit Purposeful Teaching Academy (www.purposeful247.com), follow @sheldoneakins on Instagram and X, and listen to his podcast, *Leading Equity*, on your favorite podcast listening station.

www.ingramcontent.com/pod-product-compliance
Lightning Source LLC
Chambersburg PA
CBHW050340010526
44119CB00049B/632